To my wife, Barbara

# NORTH PACIFIC STUDIES SERIES

# CONTENTS

# ILLUSTRATIONS

"... y fué que le pareció convenible y necesario, así para el aumento de su honra como para el servicio de su república, hacerse caballero andante, y irse por todo el mundo . . . a buscar las aventuras y a ejercitarse en todo aquello que él había leído que los caballeros andantes se ejercitaban, deshaciendo todo género de agravio, y poniéndose en ocasiones y peligros donde, acabándolos, cobrase eterno nombre y fama."

"... and it appeared to him fitting and necessary, in order to increase his honor as well as serve his country, to become a knight-errant, and to go throughout the world . . . in search of adventures, putting into practice all that he had read about what knights-errant used to practice, righting every manner of wrong, and placing himself in situations and dangers where, with their conclusion, his name and fame would live forever."

Miguel de Cervantes
*Don Quixote*
Part One, Chapter 1

# FOREWORD

An English translation of the *Diario* of Bruno de Hezeta y Dudagoitia is long overdue. The celebrated Basque mariner, who is forever linked with the Northwest Coast of America, suffered bad timing insofar as publications resulting from his maritime achievements are concerned. In Herbert Beals, the brave sailor has found an informed, wise and sympathetic translator. Hitherto the praise and glory Hezeta earned has been grudgingly given, and—more particularly—the accomplishments of Hezeta and his seamen for nationalistic reasons have often been misinterpreted or downgraded. This even though Hezeta rose to become a lieutenant general (admiral) in Spain's European fleet in the glory days of El Ferrol, La Coruña and Trafalgar.

Herbert Beals' superb translation and historical overview marks the seventh volume in the North Pacific Studies of Western Imprints, The Press of The Oregon Historical Society.

It is welcome on many points. Certainly among them must be the sidelight thrown on aspects of Russian penetration of the Pacific, the long-identified Spanish lake—born of the Treaty of Tordesillas—flowing toward the boundless northern horizons.

As well, Beals' translation gives glory to the astonishing energies of the Spaniards' navigators and land travelers doggedly moving north under the baleful eyes of ever-changing but always impatient viceroys enthroned in Mexico City. Historians who have walked over the now vacant flatlands where the busy shipyards of San Blas once hummed must wonder. How could this a strategic site have been so ill chosen? How in that village, amidst its swamp and malarial surround, could such a fine town be built and so substantial ship production have been achieved? The launching records certainly put the lie to any mañana philosophy. Royal scrutiny and shortages notwithstanding, it remains an impressive achievement by any standard.

This is not to say the ships were beautifully made. They were hardly the perfect work often found in French, Danish or British yards. Rough and ready as they of necessity usually were, ships from ways of San Blas and Acapulco accomplished sailing miracles. Most were cramped. Some were living hells. Others disintegrated on lonely reefs in treacherous seas and surf.

It is necessary, too, for us to reflect upon the centuries-old Iberian drive toward discovery, exploration, and glory; particularly since Spaniards and Portuguese in service were less driven by the unbelievable profits which had come to many a Russian fur hunter combing across the fog-shrouded islands and bays of the north.

Of great import for English language readers, Beals places the several Northern searches into a meaningful Spanish maritime chronology. At the same time, he nicely evaluates the accomplishments of sailors preceding Hezeta up the wild and unpredictable North American coastline. He also neatly evaluates much of the scholarship and questions that have intrigued or bewildered readers through the last century of evaluation.

While this series will include other Spanish accounts and studies of the northern expeditions, this is a notable first. An essential reason for our state of Oregon is perhaps Hezeta's link with that greatest artery of the Oregon Country, the Columbia River. There is no doubt that Hezeta and his exhausted crew in the *Santiago* did look into the mouth of the "River of the West." And it is possible that no other European sailor did so until many years later in the era of the *Jenny, Columbia* and *Chatham.* Yet Hezeta never will receive the real credit he deserves for this discovery. Preoccupation with secrecy has sometimes been as harmful to Spanish questors as it has to often forgotten Russian discoverers of North Pacific and Arctic geographic features, men who smarted as their discoveries were later formally named by successors who published their findings in other languages.

In part the intention of this growing North Pacific Studies Series is to bring back to historical recognition and perspective forgotten as well as famous ships and men. In the coming years, we hope to bring laurels and distinction to many lost and unrecognized heroes of North Pacific sagas. Always in the van will be Hezeta.

Thomas Vaughan
General Editor
North Pacific Studies Series

# PREFACE

Among the promontories on Oregon's central coast, pounded relentlessly by the Pacific surf, there is one bearing the name "Heceta Head." Westward of this point, some 30 miles to sea, the ocean swells roll across shallows known as "Heceta Bank." These names were bestowed in the 19th century by George Davidson of the U.S. Coast and Geodetic Survey to honor a Spanish navigator who noted the banks as he sailed this stretch of coast in 1775.

Despite Davidson's memorializing gesture, the name of Bruno de Hezeta is not widely known today. A change in Spanish orthography in the 19th century deprived his name of the spelling he had always used (the "z" was changed to "c"), and the few English-speaking persons familiar with his name seldom pronounced it correctly (an approximation is *Ey-they-ta*, not *Hey-kay-ta* or *Hey-say-ta*). Whether misspelled or mispronounced, it made little difference, for Hezeta's name seemed never destined to achieve the recognition it deserved.

Don Bruno was doubtless allured by the fame that great discoveries in the unknown lands of the Americas could sometimes bring. As with Hispanic explorers and *conquistadores* before him, and in the spirit of Cervantes' Don Quixote, he set forth in "search of adventures . . . placing himself in situations and in dangers where, with their conclusion, his name and fame would live forever." But it was not quite to be. The sufferings, privations and dangers he and his men endured, and the remarkable geographic discoveries they made, earned them little more than a footnote in history. This book seeks in some measure to right that wrong.

For over two centuries, Hezeta's own account of his fateful voyage has remained unpublished and untranslated into English (except for brief extracts). It seemed, therefore, time to bring this compelling story of adventure, dark tragedy and historic discovery to a wider audience. In doing this, I have received the assistance of a number of persons without whom this book would not have been possible.

Thomas Vaughan, Executive Director of the Oregon Historical Society, well knowing the importance of Hezeta's 1775 voyage, lent his enthusiastic and inspired support from the time the keel of this book was first laid.

The encouragement and advice of E.A.P. Crownhart-Vaughan, herself a recognized translator of historical documents, helped to sustain my efforts. Her gracious assistance in providing access to documents on microfilm in the Oregon Historical Society collection has been especially helpful.

I owe a large debt of gratitude to Professor Roderick Diman of the Foreign Language Department at Portland State University. He kindly took many hours from his busy schedule and patiently listened to my English rendering of Hezeta's Spanish, comparing it against the holographic texts. His comments and corrections proved invaluable, and I might never have uncovered the meaning of some of Hezeta's more obscure sentences had it not been for Professor Diman's assistance.

Terence O'Donnell of the Oregon Historical Society staff encouraged me in undertaking this project and assisted in bringing it to Mr. Vaughan's attention.

The book's design, editorial styling and production have been in the capable and talented hands of Bruce Taylor Hamilton, OHS Assistant Director and Executive Editor of Publications, Western Imprints, The Press of the Oregon Historical Society. In this task, he has been ably assisted by Colleen Compton-Campbell, Krisell M. Buxton and Stephanie A. Smith.

My wife, Barbara, typed the original draft of the manuscript. Victor Dahl, Donald Paul and Dean Schamp read the manuscript, offering a number of helpful suggestions.

Other persons have contributed in less direct but important ways. Discussions with Cornelia Cerf, a person fluent in Spanish with whom I had consulted for assistance in reading a section of

Hezeta's account, helped me to formulate this undertaking. Charles Olson allowed me to accompany him on two voyages along the Washington coast during the summers of 1978 and 1979. These were invaluable opportunities to view some of the coastline much as Hezeta had seen it, and to experience firsthand the sensation of navigating these waters in a small sailing vessel.

Finally, one cannot write of the Spanish presence on the Northwest Coast without acknowledging Henry R. Wagner. This boundlessly energetic compiler and translator of the documents of Hispanic discovery along the North American west coast left a legacy of scholarship that will not likely be exceeded. One may not always agree with his conclusions, and some have thought him overly concerned with the minutiae of history, but of the overall worth of his contribution there is no denying. For some reason, however, Hezeta's account of the 1775 expedition escaped Wagner's wide-flung net, leaving some of the joy of scholarly discovery to others. For this, I am also grateful.

# EDITORIAL PRINCIPLES

I n translating the text of Hezeta's *Diario*, every effort has been made to make his writing accessible to the modern reader. The translation remains nevertheless substantially literal, except for idiomatic expressions or where strict adherence would have produced stilted English. In some cases it has been necessary to substitute an antecedent noun for a pronoun in the interests of clarity (Hezeta sometimes uses pronouns with such abandon that their antecedent nouns are difficult to identify when translated into English, although in the Spanish they are usually clear because of the distinction of gender). Sometimes a sentence requires the insertion of a word or phrase implied by the context; such insertions are enclosed in brackets. Punctuation of the original text is completely unlike modern usage, so no attempt has been made to follow it in the translation.

Certain terms of measurement, *braza*, *vara* and *tuesa*, have not been translated into their comparable English terms ("fathom," "yard" and "two yards," respectively), since their value in Spanish during the 18th century differed somewhat from English usage. When Hezeta wrote "10 *brazas*" it is misleading to read "10 fathoms," since in fact the Spanish *braza* was only .92 fathoms. The Spanish word *arroba* has also been left untranslated since its English equivalent, "quarter weight," is so seldom used today. Although the Spanish word *pie*, meaning "foot," is not exactly equivalent to an English foot (it is 11 inches), Hezeta's references to "Parisian feet" already warn the reader that the English value for a foot is not intended. Thus, *pie* has been translated as "foot."

Other terms of measurement, *legua* and *milla*, have been translated into their comparable English terms ("league" and "mile"). It cannot be known with certainty whether Hezeta was using a marine or land league, a nautical or statute mile, or even if they were equal to modern measurements using these names. Internal evidence of the text suggests that he was using a league and mile close to the modern marine league and nautical mile. Whatever the case, no real purpose is served in retaining the Spanish terms untranslated in these cases. The reader is referred to the Glossary for a more complete explanation of each term of measurement.

Several other words have been left untranslated: *porras, balsas, aguas malas* (signs of land), *ranchería* (a small Indian village), *centenares* and *vavijunces* (species of birds). In these cases, the Spanish terms have remained untranslated because they either have no good English equivalent or their identification is uncertain. Their first occurrence in the text is footnoted with an explanation.

Certain principles have been followed in the use of Spanish place names. In the Introduction, Spanish geographic terms such as *cabo, isla, río, bahía*, et cetera, and the various names with which they are linked are neither translated nor italicized where modern toponyms have not been Anglicized (mainly in Mexico). An exception to this has been made when the initial naming of a landmark is mentioned—in which case the names are italicized or translated. For the most part, this exception concerns place names north of modern Mexico, where Spanish geographic terms have tended to be Anglicized (*cabo* to cape, *isla* to island) or Spanish place names have been supplanted entirely by English ones. Where such changes have occurred every effort has been made to identify the correspondence between Anglicized modern place names and their Spanish antecedents—in so far as that is possible.

Names mentioned in the Hezeta *Diario* that were given by the expedition to geographic features are retained in their Spanish form (italicized) followed by an English translation in brackets when they first occur in the translation text. Only the Spanish form (italicized) is used subsequently. Again, every effort has been made to identify (in the annotations) the correspondence between Hezeta's Spanish names and modern toponyms—to the extent that can be done.

Hezeta's writing differs in certain respects from modern usage, and it has its share of spelling inconsistencies. Aside from orthographic shifts that have occurred in Spanish since 1775, such as "q" to "c," "x" to "j," "s" to "z" and "z" to "c," et cetera, Hezeta used "v" and "b" interchangeably. Viceroy Bucareli's name is as often spelled with an initial "V" as not. Moreover, Hezeta's use of accents bears almost no resemblance to modern usage.

Where Spanish personal names occur in the translation, or other Spanish words or toponyms are left untranslated, certain principles have governed. Personal names follow the orthography of the manuscript sources, except that accents have been supplied in accordance with modern usage. Spelling inconsistencies have been resolved arbitrarily in favor of a single prevailing or preferred spelling—"Bucareli," for example, is used in the translation consistently in preference to "Vucareli." As for place names or other untranslated words, modern Spanish usage (spelling and accents) has been followed. The Spanish trilled "rr" in Manrrique and Monterrey, however, has been dropped in favor of the Anglicized single "r." Numbers have been spelled out or given as numerals following the Spanish text.

Finally, a word of explanation concerning dates is appropriate. When the expedition left San Blas on the evening of 16 March, Hezeta began systematically recording events in accordance with nautical or ship's time—which runs from noon to noon instead of midnight to midnight, as with civil time. Thus, for example, events occurring between noon, 16 March, and noon, 17 March, were grouped under the same diary entry. He followed this procedure (more or less) until 9 June, when the expedition went ashore at Trinidad Harbor. At that point, without explanation, his daily entries changed to civil time reckoning, becoming progressively less systematic—possibly because of the hardships its author later endured.

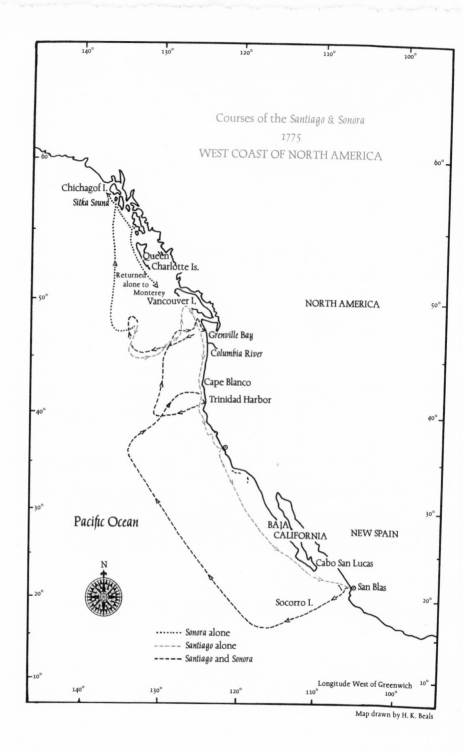

Courses of the *Santiago* & *Sonora*
1775
WEST COAST OF NORTH AMERICA

Chichagof I.
Sitka Sound

Queen
Charlotte Is.

Returned
alone to
Monterey
Vancouver I.

NORTH AMERICA

Grenville Bay

Columbia River

Cape Blanco

Trinidad Harbor

Pacific Ocean

N

BAJA
CALIFORNIA

NEW SPAIN

Cabo San Lucas

San Blas

Socorro I.

........ *Sonora* alone
------- *Santiago* alone
------ *Santiago* and *Sonora*

Longitude West of Greenwich

Map drawn by H. K. Beals

# FOR HONOR AND COUNTRY
## INTRODUCTION

The reverse design of Spanish American coinage in the 18th century (previous page). The pillars symbolize the Straits of Gibraltar (known in the ancient world as the Pillars of Hercules). The two hemispheres represent the Old and New Worlds under the Spanish crown. Inscribed on the banner entwining the pillars are the Latin words *plus ultra* (more beyond). This alludes to Columbus' discovery disproving the ancient belief that there was no more beyond—*non plus ultra*—the Pillars of Hercules.

# INTRODUCTION

On 29 August 1775, a weatherworn frigate, five-and-one-half months out of the Spanish naval base at San Blas on the west coast of Mexico, emerged from the California coastal mist and dropped anchor at four in the afternoon in the sheltered waters of Monterey Bay. The faces of the officers and men all bore the effects of their ordeal at sea, for exhaustion and sickness had come to be their unrelenting companions throughout much of the voyage. Even at this moment of deliverance, one sailor, Antonio Esteban, died while being carried ashore. Yet, by their sacrifices they had helped to dispel some of the mystery that had hitherto shrouded one of the earth's last temperate coastlines to be explored by Europeans.

Accounts of this and other early Spanish maritime expeditions to the Northwest Coast of America have never achieved the fame they deserve among English-speaking audiences. This neglect may have been due in part to the official secrecy in which such voyages were often originally cloaked, but language and cultural differences have also played a role. The underlying Hispanic thread in Pacific Northwest history has come to be recognized only gradually and imperfectly by Anglo-Americans. New Englander Robert Gray, for instance, is commonly credited with discovering the Columbia River in 1792, yet Spanish navigators had in fact sighted the same river 17 years earlier. Some popular English-language accounts of North American exploration do not mention the two voyages that brought back word of the first European glimpses of that river and the coastline stretching between California and Alaska.

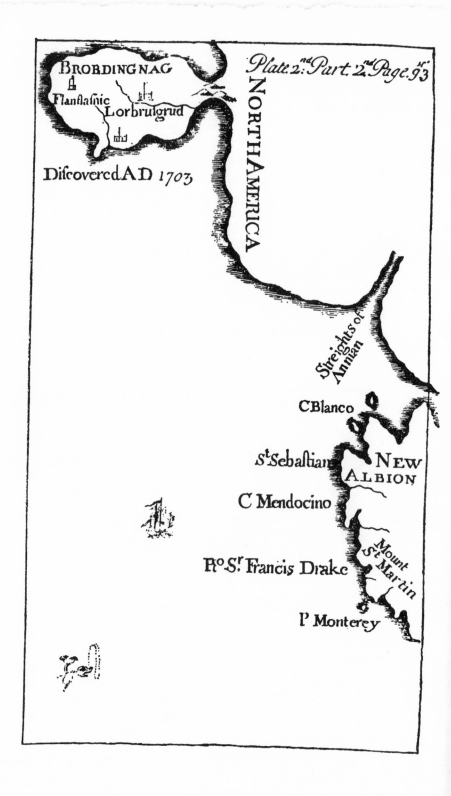

BRODDINGNAG

Flanflafnic

Lorbrulgrud

Difcovered AD 1703

NORTH AMERICA

Plate 2.nd Part. 2.nd Page. 93

Streights of Annian

C Blanco

St Sebaftian

NEW ALBION

C Mendocino

Mount St Martin

Pto Sr Francis Drake

P Monterey

4

The story of the second of these expeditions, as seen through the eyes of its commander, is told in the accompanying translation of Bruno de Hezeta's *Diario*. It is an eyewitness account of events having considerable significance in the early exploration of the Pacific Northwest. Important as they are, however, these events are only part of a long Hispanic struggle to penetrate the mysteries of the northeastern Pacific rim. The voyage was part of a revival of exploring interests that had originated more than two-and-one-half centuries earlier, and it is within this context that an understanding of the expedition commanded by Hezeta in 1775 is best approached.

## THE NORTHERN MYSTERY

When Jonathan Swift sought a locale for the second of the lands visited by Lemuel Gulliver, he chose the northwestern coast of North America. The mythical country of Brobdingnag, as he called it, could be placed with impunity on a map anywhere north of Cape Mendocino—allowing a little space for the semi-legendary capes Blanco and San Sebastián—because in 1726, the year *Gulliver's Travels* appeared, there was no reliable information to refute it. Gulliver's description of the "discovery" of Brobdingnag sounds authentic, although it was in fact the creation of Swift's inventive mind:

On the 16th day of June, 1703, a boy on the topmast discovered land. On the 17th we came in full view of a great island or continent (for we knew not whether), on the south side whereof was a small neck of land jutting out into the sea, and a creek too shallow to hold a ship of above one hundred tons. We cast anchor within a league of this creek, and our captain sent a dozen of his men well armed in the longboat, with vessels for water.[1]

When these words were being penned, over a century had

Map (opposite) appearing in Jonathan Swift's *Gulliver's Travels* (1726), depicting the mythical country of Brobdingnag on the northwestern coast of North America. It demonstrates the nearly complete ignorance of this coast among Europeans in the early 18th century.

(From Jonathan Swift, *Gulliver's Travels and Other Writings*, ed. by Louis A. Landa, 1960. OHS neg. #73217) passed since the last European ship had set out purposely to explore the northern coasts that Sir Francis Drake had called Nova Albion, but which the Spanish knew as Alta California. That effort, the expedition of Sebastián Vizcaíno in 1602–03, had been the culmination of a series of Spanish exploratory probes northward, which had begun in the mid-16th century. The motivations underlying these expeditions varied from time to time, but they seldom if ever were organized and sent out merely for reasons of sheer curiosity. Such voyages were costly, arduous and risky, requiring both considerable effort and raw courage, to say nothing of the consummate sailing skills necessary to gain latitude on a coast where contrary northwesters commonly blow.

No less a figure than Hernando Cortés put in motion the first maritime efforts to explore the North American Pacific coast from Mexico northward. These were enterprises avowedly in search of wealth, but they also seemed to have been motivated by hopes that a waterway linking the Gulf of Mexico and the Pacific would be found.[2] Cortés established a shipbuilding industry on the Pacific side of the Isthmus of Tehuantepec from which he launched his northward sea expeditions beginning in 1532. Initially, his efforts met with extraordinary bad luck. Adding to the normal difficulties of such voyages, one of his principal rivals, Nuño de Guzmán, had established himself strategically on the Mexican coast at a place called Culiacán, effectively denying shelter to ships moving northward into the Gulf of California. The first of Cortés' northern ventures, commanded by Diego Hurtado de Mendoza, came to a tragic end somewhere in the waters north of Culiacán.

In 1533, a second expedition was sent out in which two newly constructed ships quickly became separated, each coming to very different fates. The *San Lázaro*, under Hernando de Grijalva, seems to have been driven westerly out into the Pacific, where an island was discovered and given the name Santo Tomás (probably Isla Socorro in the Revillagigedo group of modern charts). The ship then returned to the Mexican coast in the vicinity of the present state of Colima, eventually making it back to Acapulco. The second ship, the *Concepción*, was not so fortunate. That ship's crew mutinied under leadership of a pilot named Fortún Ximénez de Bertandoña, and its captain, Diego de Becerra, was killed. With Ximénez in command, the ship pushed northward, reaching what was thought to be an island, where most of the crew (including Ximénez) were killed in an encounter with natives. A few survivors escaped to reach the mainland, only to be seized by Guzmán.[3]

News of the fate of the *Concepción* eventually reached Cortés because one of the sailors managed to escape from Guzmán's hands. The story told by that survivor apparently was sufficiently sprinkled with mention of gold and pearls to induce Cortés in 1535 to lead personally an expedition to locate and occupy the supposed island found by Ximénez. Although documentation of this venture is scanty, Henry R. Wagner believes that Cortés' ships put in at Bahía de La Paz on the southeastern coast of Baja California,[4] and Samuel E. Morison flatly asserts this to be "*the* discovery of California."[5] While this may slight the contribution of the mutineer Ximénez, there is little question that from this time on a major new geographic feature—whether an island or peninsula was then still unclear—entered the Spanish conception of the Pacific coast north of Culiacán.

Not long after Cortés had established himself at La Paz, another event occurred that profoundly influenced Spanish thinking about what lay north of Mexico. In March 1536 four half-naked figures appeared on the banks of the Río Sinaloa, about 90 miles north of Culiacán, with the incredible tale that they were survivors of an ill-fated expedition that had vanished on the west coast of Florida nine years earlier. Claiming to have reached the Texas coast in a small boat, they told of having gradually worked their way overland across the northern periphery of Mexico and down the Pacific coast. Their names were Alonzo del Castillo, Andrés Dorantes, Estevanico and Alvar Núñez Cabeza de Vaca, names that quickly became associated with a story about "emeralds . . . brought from some lofty mountains that stand toward the north, where were populous towns and very large houses."[6] This tale would lead eventually to the famous expedition of Francisco Vázquez de Coronado in 1540 to find the Seven Cities of Cíbola,[7] although, as Wagner suggests, "all the expeditions to the north in the ensuing six years may be justly considered as having been brought about by this story."[8]

It might seem odd that in searching for fabled cities thought to be somewhere northward in the mountains there would be a spur to coastal exploration. But accurate geographical conceptions of the lands above Mexico were yet to be formulated, and there was no particular reason to rule out the possibility that the western coastline might turn eastward at some point, offering maritime access to Cíbola's supposed seven fabulous cities. Thus, among the expeditions sent out on this search by sea, one in particular would contribute significantly to understanding the true nature of Cortés' discovery at Bahía de La Paz (or Santa Cruz as he called it).

Cortés was forced to abandon the La Paz settlement in 1537, returning to Mexico City under orders of the newly appointed viceroy of New Spain, Antonio de Mendoza, who was determined to end such private ventures. Cortés' west coast interests were nevertheless maintained under the command of Francisco de Ulloa, who in 1539 set out with three ships from Acapulco to press on with the search by sea for Cabeza de Vaca's purported "populous towns."[9] One of the ships, the *Santo Tomás*, was taken into custody by the viceroy's men at Guatulco after a storm forced it to seek refuge; but the other two, the *Santa Aqueda* and *Trinidad*, managed to sail up the Gulf of California to the mouth of the Colorado River. They returned south along the east coast of Baja California to Cabo San Lucas at its southern tip, where they doubled the cape and headed northward along the outer littoral of what they then must have realized was a peninsula. The two ships continued up the coast and in January 1540, they reached a group of three islands in latitude 28°N, the largest of which they called *Isla de Cedros*. From that vicinity, the *Santa Aqueda* is known to have returned south on 5 April with Ulloa's narrative of the voyage,[10] while the *Trinidad*, with the expedition's commander aboard, proceeded north alone. No account of Ulloa's return voyage in the *Trinidad* has survived, but Wagner believes he may have reached 32° or 33°N (the vicinity of present San Diego),[11] while Morison is inclined to think Ulloa went no higher than 30°N.[12] Whatever the truth, although nothing resembling Vaca's towns was seen, Ulloa had shown that California was no island and that the path to northern discoveries lay along its outer coast.

By 1541, Coronado had returned from his journey through the modern states of Arizona, New Mexico, Texas, Oklahoma and Kansas with the discouraging news that Cíbola was merely a collection of pueblos. Nevertheless, he had learned of another fabled place called "Quivira," which was thought to have been located in the plains of what is now central Kansas. This new chimera of the north, described by one of Coronado's Indian guides, was also associated with a great river (probably the Mississippi-Missouri). However, Pedro de Castañeda's narrative of the Coronado expedition mistakenly placed Quivira "to the west . . . nearer the mountains toward the sea",[13] an error that was perpetuated on European maps of North America well into the 18th century. Wagner believes that Viceroy Mendoza may have even entertained the idea that the great river of Quivira in fact emptied into the Pacific,[14] which conceivably influenced his decision to send out the first expedition that would truly begin the maritime penetration of the "Northern Mystery"—to use the expression coined by Henry Oak.[15]

## THE CABRILLO-FERRER EXPEDITION

Mendoza commissioned Juan Rodríguez Cabrillo, a veteran soldier of the Mexican conquests, to lead a sea expedition up the outer coast of California in 1542, with the intent of pushing northward beyond Ulloa's tentative probe in that direction. The objectives of this voyage, insofar as they can be gleaned from the surviving accounts,[16] seem to have involved a search for some great river and a painstaking interest in ascertaining names of the native settlements encountered. Considering these aims, a reasonable surmise is that the underlying motivation of the expedition may well have been to find Quivira, even if no explicit avowal of such a purpose has come to light.

The expedition set out from Navidad, just north of Colima, on 27 June 1542, with two ships, the *San Salvador* and *Victoria*, bound for Cabo San Lucas and the outer coast of Baja California. They successfully reached Ulloa's Isla de Cedros and pushed on northward, where near the end of September they discovered "a very good closed port . . . which they named 'San Miguel'."[17] They landed and took possession of the harbor (now San Diego Bay), making friendly contact with the native inhabitants. Continuing up the coast, the expedition found itself amidst numerous and often well-constructed Indian settlements on the mainland and on a series of islands lying offshore. Here Cabrillo recorded the names of more than 40 native towns, built by the remarkable Chumash people of

9

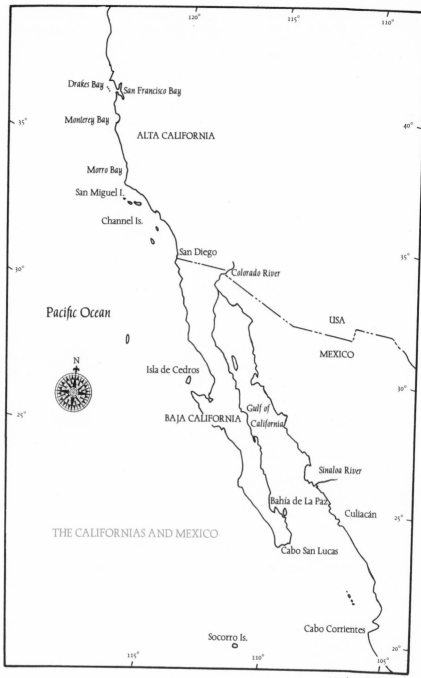

120°  115°  110°

Drakes Bay ·. ⸜San Francisco Bay

35°  Monterey Bay  40°

ALTA CALIFORNIA

Morro Bay

San Miguel I.

Channel Is.

San Diego  35°

30°  Colorado River

Pacific Ocean  USA

N  MEXICO

Isla de Cedros  30°

25°  BAJA CALIFORNIA  Gulf of California

Sinaloa River

Bahía de La Paz

Culiacán  25°

THE CALIFORNIAS AND MEXICO

Cabo San Lucas

Cabo Corrientes  20°

Socorro Is.

115°  110°  105°

Map drawn by H. K. Beals

the Channel Islands area.[18] An unavailing search also was begun off the mainland north of the Santa Barbara Channel for "a large river . . . of which they had information."[19] Off the Big Sur coast they instead encountered a fearsome November storm that eventually drove them northward to a prominent pine-covered cape that they located in latitude 40°N, naming it *Cabo de Pinos*. This latitude corresponds roughly to forested Cape Mendocino (lat. 40°26'N), and Donald C. Cutter suggests that that may in fact have been what they saw.[20] Wagner, however, believes it was Point Reyes (lat. 38°N) just northwest of the Golden Gate, in spite of the fact that it is treeless, because of Cabrillo's tendency to observe latitudes for known locations between 1 degree and 2 degrees too high.[21]

Whatever northerly extreme that autumnal storm may have carried them, by 16 November the expedition had returned southward where "they arrived off a large *ensenada*"[22] and anchored, according to the narrative, in 45 fathoms. Morison thought this *ensenada* probably was Drakes Bay behind Point Reyes, but if the account correctly states the depth of their anchorage, it was more likely Monterey Bay.[23] In any event, they called it *Bahía de los Pinos* because of its pine forest. Heavy surf prevented them from going ashore, so they returned south to winter at the windward-most of the Channel Islands (today called San Miguel Island, although their name for it was *Isla de Posesión*). While there, on 3 January 1543, Cabrillo died, apparently from an infected broken arm that he had suffered earlier in the same vicinity.[24] Command of the expedition thus devolved upon chief pilot Bartolomé Ferrer (or Ferrelo), who was enjoined by his dying captain to continue exploring the coast.

On 18 February, the expedition, under its new commander, set out to relocate Cabo de Pinos, which they did within a week. After having run from there northwesterly, they observed their latitude at 43°N on 28 February, and when they were finally forced to turn back in the face of a furious northwester, "they believed that they were in 44°."[25] These latitudes, if accurate, would have placed the ships off the southern Oregon coast, but with the possibility of an error as much as 2 degrees there is little certainty of this. While they were buffeted about in these northern waters, the narrative says that indications were seen of "a very large river of which they had heard much."[26] Thus, while no such great river had actually been found, the idea of its existence was kept alive as an inducement for pursuit by subsequent navigators. Both ships, although temporarily separated and subjected to continued severe weather, eventually made it back to Navidad on 15 April 1543.

The Cabrillo-Ferrer expedition is a landmark event in the exploration of the Pacific's northeastern rim, not only for its display of dauntless courage, but because it accomplished the first reconnaissance of a coastline possessing some of the the best harbors in western North America. Only a handful of these ports were actually visited, and the finest of all, San Francisco Bay, remained undiscovered. But the advantages of Alta California to future navigation were substantially revealed, and many of the geographic misconceptions of it dispelled—or at least pushed northward. Unfortunately, these objectives appear not to have been the main reason for the voyage, and with no evidence of glistening, wealthy cities, official interest waned, allowing the results of Cabrillo's efforts to slip into obscurity.

## THE MANILA-ACAPULCO TRADE

Spanish subjugation of the Philippines was initiated by the Miguel López de Legazpi expedition in 1564–65, which embarked from the same port (Navidad) that Cabrillo had used. This expedition opened a far more reliable means of tapping the wealth of exotic civilizations than continued ventures to find rumored cities in the northern wilds of America. From the outpost created at Manila, the Spanish would have access to a wide range of prized Asian commodities, particularly from China, including silk, tea, spices, porcelain, gold, ivory, pearls, rubies, sapphires and a list of other valuables so numerous that, in Antonio de Morga's words, "to recount all of which could mean never finishing, nor would even masses of paper suffice for the task."[27] There were also many less exalted supplies needed in New Spain, such as cotton cloth, kettles, nails, needles, thread, beeswax and gunpowder, that were readily available in the Orient. A sailing route westward, utilizing the equitorial trade winds, from New Spain by which Mexican silver could be carried to the Philippines for payment was already well-established. All that was needed for a lucrative commerce to develop was to find an equally dependable route for cargo-laden ships to return to New Spain.

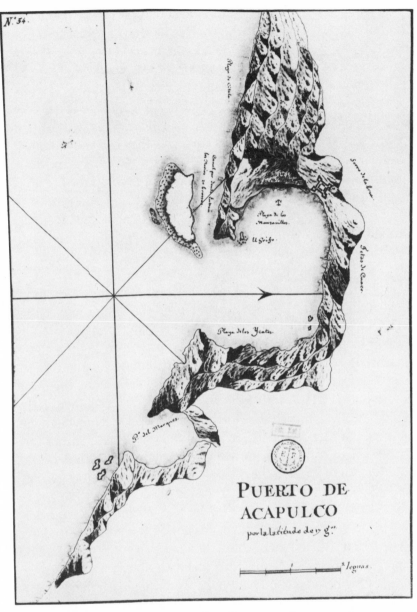

PUERTO DE
ACAPULCO

por la latitude de 19 g.ª

A map of the harbor at Acapulco of uncertain date. From this point the Manila galleons embarked on their westward voyages across the Pacific, stopping over at Guam before they reached the Philippines. Returning across the North Pacific to California, they proceeded south along the North American coast, burdened with Oriental riches, seeking this splendid anchorage.

(OHS neg.#68749)

Such a return route was located the same year Legazpi secured a foothold in the Philippines when one of his ships, the *San Pablo* captained by his grandson Felipe de Salcedo, utilized the westerlies in the vicinity of latitude 40°N to make the eastward crossing. The route followed carried the ship to the Californias at about latitude 34°N where, according to Wagner, a landfall was made at the very same island (San Miguel) that Cabrillo had wintered 22 years earlier. On the way southward from Alta California they had the prevailing coastal northwesterlies astern, so that by 1 October 1565, four months out of the Philippines, the *San Pablo* arrived on the Mexican coast off Navidad. Salcedo then decided to put in farther south at the better harbor of Acapulco. The rigors of the voyage were attested by the fact that 16 crewmen had died, including chief pilot Esteban Rodríguez, and that the rest were all sick. But the way eastward across the North Pacific was now known.[28]

From that year forward, for two-and-one-half centuries, most Spanish ships with Asian commodities plied this same route. These were the Manila galleons or *naos de China* which departed Manila in June or by mid-July, sailing northeastward past Japan to the vicinity of latitude 40°N, where they turned east, bound for the Californias. The final leg of the voyage was southeasterly along the coast to Acapulco, which with luck was reached by December. They would usually approach the North American coast somewhere between Cape Mendocino (lat. 40°26′ N) and the Channel Islands (lat. 34°N), where their pilots learned to recognize the nearness of the land by *señas* or signs on the ocean's surface, such as floating jellyfish or kelp, known to occur at certain distances from the coast.[29] These *señas* were always welcomed for they meant the voyage was nearing its conclusion, but the seacoast itself was greatly feared. Its hazardous uncharted rocks, shoals, headlands and reefs were forbidding under the best of conditions, and with a heavy sea running or a pall of fog no pilot in his right mind would approach the land any closer than was absolutely necessary to guide his course southward. Knowledge of a temporary safe harbor after the long and arduous North Pacific run would have been welcome, but the galleon captains were no more eager than the pilots to risk their exhausted crews or valuable cargoes by closing with the coast to conduct exploring operations.

It is remarkable that the Manila ships struggled for many years on their Pacific crossings apparently without any knowledge of the superb harbor at San Diego, the haven at Monterey Bay, or even Cabrillo's winter anchorage at San Miguel Island. Nor was much official interest shown at first in mounting new expeditions to Alta California. Evidently, the problems of the Manila-Acapulco run were irksome only to the crews and passengers who actually faced what was called "the longest, most tedious and most dangerous voyage in all the seas."[30] Whatever other difficulties there may have been, Spanish control of the Pacific precluded worries of foreign attempts to intercept these richly laden ships, which seems to have also contributed to official complacency.

## THE FOREIGN MENACE: DRAKE AND CAVENDISH

This all changed suddenly in 1578 when Francis Drake burst unexpectedly on the Pacific scene. This bold English mariner, passing through the Straits of Magellan, proceeded up the coast where he spread havoc among unprotected Spanish settlements and shipping from Chile to Mexico. His depredations made it clear enough to the Spanish court that the Pacific was no longer secure from foreign intrusion; but also the unusual manner in which he managed to elude capture created a new and urgent reason for the Spanish to renew exploration on the Alta California coast. Drake sailed out of Guatulco, his final Mexican stop just below Acapulco, in April 1579. He was bound for the northern coasts to look briefly for the rumored Straits of Anian or, if that proved fruitless, to find a harbor for careening his ship, the *Golden Hind*, before attempting a westward crossing of the Pacific. From some captured Spanish charts and sailing directions he apparently was warned that any attempt to head directly up the coast would require beating against the prevailing northwesters. He thus set a "course directly into the sea . . . to get a winde"[31] which by June carried him at least as high as the Cabrillo expedition had reached under Ferrer in 1543—and probably higher, at least to latitude 43°N and possibly as high as the vicinity of 48°N.

The details of Drake's famous sojourn on the Alta California coast, or Nova Albion as he called it, have been endlessly debated, with few conclusive results.[32] But from the standpoint of assessing its impact on Spanish thinking, the details are relatively unimportant because the Spanish themselves had only the sketchiest idea as to where Drake had actually gone. Aside from knowing that April was too late in the season to make a safe westward crossing of the Pacific immediately, the only definite information available to the Spanish concerning Drake's possible intention to go north was the testimony of Núño de Silva. This Portuguese pilot, captured by Drake in the Cape Verde Islands, had been pressed into service until he was set free at Guatulco. In depositions taken from Silva by the Spanish, they learned that, "While in Guatulco Drake took out a map and pointed out on it how he had to return by a strait which is in 66° and that if he did not find it, then by way of China."[33]

The implications of such a northern penetration by Drake, particularly if it actually revealed the existence of a strait connecting the Pacific with the North Atlantic, were potentially alarming to the Spanish because of its relationship to the route of the eastbound Manila galleons. Foreign ships freely prowling the northeastern waters of the Pacific would constitute a serious menace to the lucrative commerce linking Mexico and the Orient. While the Spanish response was neither swift nor merely a reaction to Drake's exploits, the 1584 appointment of Archbishop Pedro Moya de Contreras as viceroy of New Spain seems to have heralded a concern for the problems of the Manila-Acapulco navigation. In January 1585, Moya wrote Philip II in Madrid:

When the ships come from China, they sight the coast of New Spain 700 leagues before reaching Acapulco, and from there sail almost in sight of land. Although it may be necessary to land to repair the ships, or to take on a supply of water or other things, they cannot do so as the ports on all that coast are not known, nor have they any place in which to take shelter from the contrary winds which ordinarily blow in that quarter. . . . In order that all this may come to an end, and your Majesty may have knowledge of all that coast which some say runs on to join the mainland of China, and others that it terminates in a strait called "Anian" which continues to and ends near Ireland, I have ordered two *fragatas* built to search for and discover all the ports, islands, rivers, mountains and settlements which there are or may be on all that coast.[34]

Before construction of the two ships could get under way, however, Moya was presented with an alternate plan by a shadowy figure named Francisco Gali, whose exact connection with the Manila-Acapulco trade is uncertain. Gali's proposal was to launch the expedition from the Philippines instead of northward from Mexico, and, in so doing, he seems to have had his eye on locating the alluring but mythical North Pacific Armenian Isles. Moya was persuaded to support his scheme, and Gali reached the Philippines by June 1585 only to die before the expedition could embark.[35]

Gali was succeeded by Pedro de Unamuno, another figure about whom even less is known, to carry out the planned expedition. After considerable delay, the frigate *Nuestra Señora de Esperanza* commenced the voyage from Macao in July 1587. Unamuno proceeded to the North Pacific where he spent much futile time in search of the Armenian Isles and two other equally imaginary places called *Rica de Oro* (rich in gold) and *Rica de Plata* (rich in silver). Giving up this hunt, which may have been the real motivation of the voyage, he headed for the Californias where he anchored on 18 October in a harbor he called *Puerto de San Lucas*. Wagner tentatively located this port at Morro Bay (lat. 35° 20′ N), but more recent opinion suggests it may have been farther up the coast at Santa Cruz on the north side of Monterey Bay.[36] After spending three days ashore, skirmishing with the natives, and perfunctorily checking out the harbor and its surroundings, he sailed away southward to Mexico. Thus, Unamuno's sole contribution to understanding the geography of the Alta California coast was the discovery of a single vaguely located port.[37]

On 12 November, as he proceeded southward toward Acapulco, Unamuno encountered a launch near Cabo Corrientes on the central Mexican coast (in the modern state of Jalisco). This launch was searching for Unamuno's ship and the Manila galleon *Santa Ana*, also expected to arrive presently from the Orient, to warn them that an English corsair was on the coast. Unamuno's little frigate—probably not over 50 tons—was thus duly warned and safely sailed into Acapulco 10 days later. The 700-ton *Santa Ana*, however, was not so lucky. On 14 November 1587, two days after Unamuno had

17

met the launch, the lumbering Manila galleon hove in sight off Cabo San Lucas where it was attacked by English ships *Desire* and *Content*, under the command of Thomas Cavendish. It took several hours of combat to subdue the great ship, following which more than a week was required to loot its immense and valuable cargo.[38]

This humiliating and economically damaging disaster—merchants were ruined and a temporary depression is said to have gripped New Spain—should have quickly produced Spanish counter measures to tighten security along the Californias. But by the summer of 1588, the Great Armada, sent to deal with the English in their home waters, had suffered an even more disastrous defeat. As a consequence, Spain's resources were insufficient to support an immediate resumption of exploring activities.[39] Nevertheless, Cavendish had supplied the Spanish with all the reasons needed to press for more information on the ports, harbors and possible straits north of Baja California.

It is possible, as Warren Cook has suggested, that in the years immediately following the loss of the *Santa Ana*, efforts to explore northward may have been mounted which were abortive, kept secret or for which documentation has been lost.[40] Certainly, the best known of these cases is the story attributed to a Greek pilot named Apostolos Valerianos, or as he was called in Spanish, Juan de Fuca.

According to an account published in England in 1625, this mysterious figure was supposed to have found "a broad Inlet of Sea, between 47° and 48° of Latitude" during a voyage alleged to have occurred in 1592.[41] Fuca claimed to have been aboard the *Santa Ana*, losing "sixtie thousand Duckets, of his owne goods" in the Cavendish raid, and that afterward he participated in two exploring missions on the northern coasts. The first expedition was said to have been aborted because the captain's aberrant behavior caused a mutiny; but the second, under Fuca's charge, supposedly succeeded in finding not only a "broad Inlet" but a land "very fruitful, and rich of gold, Silver, Pearle, and other things." This has obvious overtones of earlier fabled but imaginary places, and the suspicion remains that Fuca's story was fabricated, even if good reasons existed to send out just such an expedition. Its veracity aside, the episode is nevertheless important because of the influence it had on subsequent explorers who were still looking in the late 18th century for the strait Fuca had supposedly found.

Of one expedition in the decade following the *Santa Ana* debacle enough is known to be fully confident of its reality. This was the voyage sponsored by Luis de Velasco, viceroy of New Spain, in compliance with a Royal Order of 17 January 1593 requiring that a search be conducted to locate safe harbors along the Manila trade route.[42] The man selected as its captain and chief pilot, Sebastián Rodrígues Cermeño, was well qualified for the task, as he apparently had been the pilot of the *Santa Ana* in 1587.[43] Like the Unamuno expedition, this would be another attempt to explore the Alta California coast by sailing out of the Philippines more or less on the eastward track of the Manila ships. But Cermeño, instead of chasing after imaginary islands, would be given "remuneration in the way of taking on board merchandise,"[44] thus combining an authorized commercial venture with the official exploring mission of the voyage.

Cermeño sailed out of the Philippines on the *San Agustín* in mid-July 1595, and although bad weather produced a rather late start, he reached the California coast in surprisingly good time. By 4 November a landfall was made at a point the narrative says was 42° N, within sight of what it calls Cabo Mendocino,[45] but which was probably either Rocky Point (lat. 41° 08′ N), near Trinidad Head, or Point St. George (lat. 41° 47′ N).[46] The next day, he proceeded to enter what Wagner believed was the harbor behind Trinidad Head. The lookouts, however, sighted some "dangerous rocks where the ship would have to anchor,"[47] which frightened them off. Cermeño nevertheless seems to have been determined to accomplish his exploring mission, giving orders to run close-in along the coast as they proceeded southward—much to the considerable consternation of his officers. On 6 November they came upon "a point of high land . . . which revealed a great *ensenada*,"[48] offering good prospects for an anchorage. It was in this bay that they finally cast anchor, landed and, according to the narrative, "took possession of the land and port in the name of the King."[49]

In all likelihood this bay, which they named *Bahía de San Francisco*, was what is today called Drakes Bay in the lee of Point Reyes (lat. 38° N) lying to the northwest of the Golden Gate. This harbor has been the subject of intense interest because there are many circumstantial indications it may have been the site of Francis Drake's anchorage in 1579.[50] But, unlike the theoretical landing of Drake, Cermeño's sojourn there would leave its imprint in a rather more substantive manner, for near the end of November, while the *San Agustín* was riding at anchor, it was wrecked in a storm. This event left the crew temporarily as castaways and the valuable cargo of Asian merchandise deposited along the beach. Three-and-one-half centuries later, 16th-century Chinese porcelain shards would be dug from nearby Miwok Indian sites, testifying to Cermeño's misfortune.[51]

Left with only a launch, which had been carried for the purpose of close-in coastal surveying, the expedition's members used it in a desperate gamble to avoid permanent stranding in Alta California. They called the launch *San Buenaventura*, and sailed away with a food supply of acorns, hazelnuts and thistles provided by the local Miwok Indians. While their voyage southward was accompanied by sickness—no doubt from being unaccustomed to such a diet—and later the specter of starvation, they managed to reach New Spain with the story of their ordeal in January 1596. Their epic voyage of survival, however, could not conceal the fact that the expedition had been nearly a complete failure. Its commercial enterprise lay scattered and abandoned in the surf of a remote northern bay, and precious little new information had been gleaned about the usefulness of this or any other such bay as shelter for the Manila galleons. The need for a different approach to exploring and charting the harbors of Alta California was now plainly and painfully obvious.

## THE VIZCAÍNO EXPEDITION

Hardly had the news of the *San Agustín*'s loss reached the viceroy in Mexico City—who was now Gaspar de Zúñiga, conde de Monterey—than plans were underway to return northward employing fresh methods. For one thing, the new viceroy was determined to end the practice of relying on private expeditions, motivated by commercial gain, as a means of attaining the crown's purposes.[52] He was equally committed to launching the next expedition up the coast from New Spain. Recalling the fate of the *San Agustín*, Monterey wrote the King: "To all practical men it seemed that in making this exploration the better method would have been for the ship to sail from here [New Spain] and along the coast."[53] Sailors experienced in beating windward up the coast might have taken exception to the viceroy's remarks; apparently Drake's method of gaining latitude by swinging far to the west had not yet come into use by Spanish mariners.[54] Still, the earlier failures of Unamuno and Cermeño argued strongly for the viceroy's position.

Sebastián Vizcaíno, veteran soldier, adventurer and occasional entrepreneur in Baja California pearling ventures, was selected to lead conde de Monterey's planned expedition. With a wary eye on his appointee's earlier involvement in the pearl business, the viceroy warned him—under no less a penalty than death—to stay out of the Gulf of California, at least until the charting of the outer coast was complete.[55] In other respects he seems to have enjoyed the viceroy's confidence, and after the usual delays the expedition embarked from Acapulco on 5 May 1602.[56] It was led by Vizcaíno's 200-ton flagship *San Diego*, and included two smaller vessels, the *Santo Tomás* and a frigate called the *Tres Reyes*. The mission of the expedition was clearly and principally the charting of harbors that would be suitable to shelter distressed Manila galleons.

They set sail on essentially the same track Cabrillo had followed 60 years earlier, but apparently without knowledge or benefit of its results. Beating windward up the outer coast, they discovered (or rediscovered) and charted the harbors and islands of the Californias from Cabo San Lucas at the southern end of Baja California northward to a bay just below latitude 37°N, where the expedition halted temporarily in mid-December. This bay was probably the same "large *ensenada*" off which Cabrillo anchored briefly, calling it Bahía de los Pinos. Vizcaíno, unaware of the previous toponym, renamed the port in honor of the conde de Monterey, although he was also sufficiently impressed by a stand of pines to name its southern promontory *Punta de Pinos*.

While at Monterey Bay, Vizcaíno assessed the situation and determined to send the *Santo Tomás* back to New Spain with a request for "provisions, men and ammunition," dispatching also "the map, report and sailing directions concerning all I have done in said exploration to the present time."[57] The *San Diego* and *Tres Reyes* then headed north again in search of Cabo Mendocino and Cermeño's Puerto de San Francisco (Drakes Bay) in hopes of locating traces of the lost *San Agustín*. They found the point off the latter harbor on 6 January, the feast day of the Epiphany (*día de los Reyes*), but next day, in the confusion of a severe northwester, the two ships became separated.

The chief pilot of the *San Diego*, Francisco de Bolaños, had been a member of Cermeño's expedition, and thus he was able to identify the harbor definitely as the one in which the *San Agustín* had been lost. He urged Vizcaíno to enter the harbor, "claiming they had left on shore on that occasion a quantity of wax and many cases of silks, and that it might be that something of the great quantity then lost might be found on the coast."[58] The *San Diego* anchored briefly behind the point which they named Reyes (the name it still bears today), but concern for the missing *Tres Reyes* prevented them from conducting a search for the remains of the *San Agustín's* cargo.

Pushing northward again, hopeful of re-establishing contact with its consort, the *San Diego* went in search of Cabo Mendocino. A cape—probably the one named Mendocino today—hove in sight on 13 January 1603. They were now subjected to severe southeasterly winds of a major winter storm, which forced them northwestward. On 19 January the weather cleared long enough for the pilots to observe the latitude at 42°N, permitting them also to sight "a cape of white earth close to some high sierras covered with snow."[59] This feature was named *Cabo Blanco de San Sebastián*, honoring Vizcaíno's patron saint, and it may have been the same southern Oregon cape that still bears the saint's name today.[60] At this point, the crew was too sick and exhausted to continue, and with the welcome appearance of a northwester, they managed to set enough sail to run before the wind southward toward New Spain.

The *Tres Reyes*, commanded by Martín de Aguilar and piloted by Antonio Flores, was similarly swept northward by the same storm. Fray Antonio de la Ascención's secondhand report of the frigate's separate voyage says that when the weather calmed down they found themselves in 43°N latitude. "Here," his account continues, "the land makes a cape or point which was named 'Cabo Blanco,' and here the coast begins to trend to the northeast. Close to it a very copious river was discovered."[61] It is possible—though by no means certain—that they glimpsed Cape Blanco (lat. 42°50'N) of modern charts, which, being the western most extension of the Oregon coast, is the beginning of a slight northeasterly trend in the

22

coastline. The river they reported seeing, which they named *Santa Inéz*, could have been any of several streams from the Rogue River south to Humboldt Bay.[62] But whatever its location or actuality, this report would serve to revive belief in the existence of a great river or strait somewhere north of Cape Mendocino. It would later be called *Río de Martín Aguilar*, honoring the ship's commander, who (along with pilot Flores) perished sometime after the river's discovery, and it would appear under that name on European maps of this coast well into the 18th century.

Both ships eventually reached the safety of New Spain, as did the *Santo Tomás* which had returned south earlier from Monterey Bay. The idea of resupplying the expedition had evidently not proven feasible, and Vizcaíno's crew was too exhausted to exercise the option he had been given to enter the Gulf of California on the return voyage. While the ordeal of beating windward up the coast exacted a heavy toll, the expedition had nevertheless achieved some notable successes. Most harbors of any significance in the Californias—except for the elusive bay inside the Golden Gate—were located and charted with considerable accuracy. Vizcaíno believed that Monterey Bay in particular was perfectly suited as a stopover for the Manila ships, arguing for its settlement, and offering himself to lead such an undertaking.[63] Not only had the viceroy's basic aim of finding and charting harbors for the security of the Philippine trade been fulfilled, but an experienced leader was available and willing to carry out successive efforts to occupy them.

## THE LAPSE OF SPANISH INTEREST

The conde de Monterey enthusiastically pushed ahead with plans to establish a settlement at the harbor to which Vizcaíno had generously given the viceroy's name. But by March 1604, a pall of uncertainty was cast over these plans by the appointment of Juan de Mendoza y Luna, marqués de Montesclaros, to replace the conde de Monterey. The new viceroy was unconvinced that a settlement at Monterey Bay would be useful enough to justify its expense, and by a curious sort of reasoning he deduced that continued exploration and settlement of Alta California would invite—rather than reduce—foreign adventurers and corsairs on the coast. He wrote the King: "For my part I think that once it was explored and settled it would be common ground for friends and enemies where, besides finding shelter for their ships, they would find Spaniards with whom to treat for food, clothing and goods."[64] And in another letter he suggested that the imaginary islands of Rica de Oro and Rica de Plata would be better places to examine and settle, even if their exact location or very existence had yet to be determined.[65]

It may have been that the marqués de Montesclaros was resentful of his predecessor's achievements, or that he believed the Monterey project was nothing but a scheme to make Vizcaíno rich.[66] Whatever underlying reasons may have impelled him, he was notably successful in stopping the project, even in the face of crown support for it. His success was in fact so pervasive that no Spanish ship would set sail from Mexico northward on the tracks of Cabrillo and Vizcaíno until the second half of the 18th century. Certainly the difficulty of sailing windward against the prevailing northwesterlies was little inducement to undertake such voyages, and it was now well known that mid-winter southerlies were more a source of trouble than assistance. With the myth of Quivira exposed, only the idea of a possible strait, passage or great river remained to lure mariners northward in the face of such discouraging navigational obstacles. And now, with the viceroy apparently believing that the best policy was to avoid discoveries, hoping thereby to prevent foreigners from learning of them, it is small wonder that exploration on the northern coasts settled into a long period of inactivity.

After the Vizcaíno expedition, the only Spanish vessels plying the waters of the northeastern Pacific during the 17th and early 18th centuries were the Manila galleons or other ships following the same eastward track. In 1606, the flagship of the Quirós expedition, the *San Pedro y Pablo*, reached Mexico from the Solomon Islands by sailing northward until falling in with the normal eastward route of the Philippine trade, following the same course as the Manila ships down the coast from a landfall just above the Channel Islands.[67] Such ships had no particular interest in exploring the coast, much less making landings, thus most of them passed silently off shore, giving the land a wide berth.

When the Manila galleons ran into trouble off the American coast, the assistance of a settlement at Monterey would have been eagerly welcomed by their exhausted passengers and crews. A good example was the case of the *Espíritu Santo* and its consort the *Jesús María*, who were caught in a violent November storm off Cape Mendocino in 1604. The storm persisted for 12 days during which time the *Espíritu Santo* was struck by lightning, narrowly escaped being driven ashore, and reached Acapulco badly damaged only after a harrowing two-month voyage down the coast.[68] Other galleons encountering similar difficulties must not have fared so well, as a number of them vanished completely somewhere in the North Pacific. There are indications that one of these lost ships may have unintentionally landed the first Europeans on the coast above Cape Blanco. Materials characteristic of the Philippine trade have often turned up on the northern Oregon coast, including large quantities of Asian beeswax and 17th-century Chinese porcelain fragments in Tillamook Indian sites. The ship that has been considered the most likely candidate for the dubious honor of depositing them (and possibly castaway survivors) there is the galleon *San Francisco Xavier*, which left the Philippines about 1705 bound for Acapulco. It failed to arrive.[69]

To the natural hazards of navigating the North Pacific were added the persistent attempts of English and Dutch corsairs to emulate the exploits of Drake and Cavendish.[70] On the whole, such privateering efforts in the 17th century met with only limited success, and it was not until 1704 that another Manila ship found itself looking down the muzzles of an English vessel bent on its capture. In this engagement, the English privateer *St. George*, under William Dampier, found itself completely outgunned by the galleon *Rosario*, and it was lucky to escape without being taken itself. Six years later Woodes Rogers, however, would successfully capture the galleon *Encarnación* off Cabo San Lucas on New Year's Day, 1710. Yet, such incidents were relatively infrequent and they evidently were not of sufficient concern to alter Spanish policy against northward exploration.

The events that finally seem to have ended Spain's long neglect of the northern coasts came from an unexpected source, one that never figured before in Spanish calculations. Russian sovereignty had spread rapidly across the Siberian expanses during the 17th century, going mostly unnoticed in Madrid and Mexico City. But as word began filtering out of St. Petersburg of a series of Russian maritime expeditions that had penetrated eastward toward North America, Spain could no longer afford to treat the matter with indifference. The two best-known of these Russian expeditions had originated on the Kamchatka Peninsula at a place called Petropavlovsk; both having been organized and led by the Dane Vitus Bering between 1725 and 1742. Bering's second expedition, with Aleksei Chirikov sharing command, had succeeded in making several landfalls along the North American coast, the most southerly of which was at about latitude 55° 30′ N,[71] near Dixon Entrance, at about where the Alaskan Panhandle meets British Columbia. Opinion why these voyages were undertaken has usually leaned toward the view that they were in quest of geographic information about the relationship between Siberia and America.[72] Recently, a different interpretation has emerged calling attention to the probability that their mission instead may have been primarily to extend Russian sovereignty into northwestern America with the eventual aim of exploiting its natural resources.[73] The Spanish government appears to have come quickly to this same conclusion, for by 1768, reversing the policies of over a century, efforts were set in motion to colonize San Diego and Monterey all part of a general reassertion of Spanish rights in Alta California and on the coasts northward.[74]

## THE FIRST BUCARELI EXPEDITION

In support of these efforts, a new naval base was hastily established on the Mexican west coast in the modern state of Nayarit. The guiding figure in organizing and administering the port facilities, shipyards and garrison that came to be known as the Naval Department of San Blas was José de Gálvez, holder of a royal appointment as *visitador-general* to New Spain.[75] The immediate purpose of this naval base was to launch and support Franciscan missions and military garrisons at San Diego and Monterey; but by 1773 these endeavors had progressed sufficiently to permit a shifting of attention to maritime exploration high on the northern coasts. Responsibility to plan and organize an expedition for such purposes fell to the new viceroy in Mexico City, Antonio María de Bucareli y Ursúa.

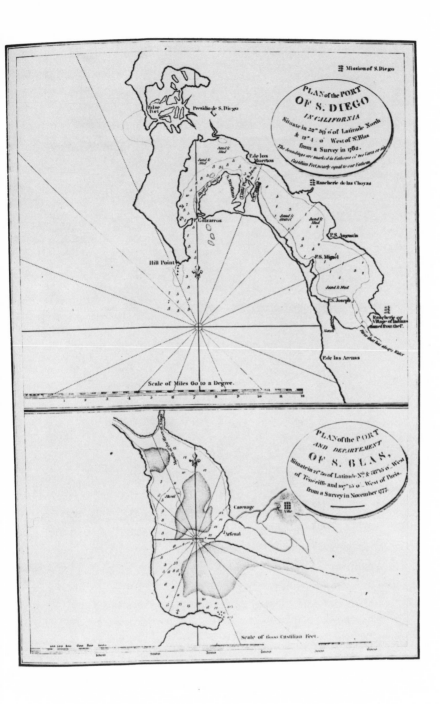

‡ Mission of S.Diego

PLAN of the PORT
OF S. DIEGO
IN CALIFORNIA
Situate in 32° 39′ 0′ of Latitude North
& 12° 4′ 0′ West of S.Blas
from a Survey in 1782.
The Soundings are marked in Fathoms of two Vares or six
Castilian Feet, nearly equal to our Fathom

Presidio de S.Diego

False Port

‡ Pt de los Muertos

‡ Rancherie de las Choyas

P.Gulzarros

P.S.Augustin

Hill Point

P.S.Miguel

P.S.Joseph

Rancherie or Village of Indians
named from the P.

Pte las Arenas

Scale of Miles 60 to a Degree.

PLAN of the PORT
AND DEPARTEMENT
OF S. BLAS,
Situate in 21° 50′ of Latitude N.° & 78°15′ 0′ West
of Teneriffe and 107° 15′ 0′ West of Paris.
from a Survey in November 1777.

Carenage

Ville

Arsenal

Shoal

Scale of 6000 Castilian Feet.

27

Maps (previous page) of the harbors at San Diego (1782) in Alta California and San Blas (1777) in Nayarit (Mexico) which were published in an English translation of La Perouse's journals. San Blas was the naval base from which the Spanish supplied their first Alta California outpost, established at San Diego in 1769. Hezeta sailed the *Santiago* out of San Blas 16 March 1775, but San Diego did not figure in the voyage because his mission was to sail far to the north of that secure harbor.

(From J.F.G. de La Pérouse, *A Voyage Round the World Performed in the Years 1785 . . . 1788 by the Boussole and Astrolabe*, Charts and Plates, 1799. OHS neg. #67567)

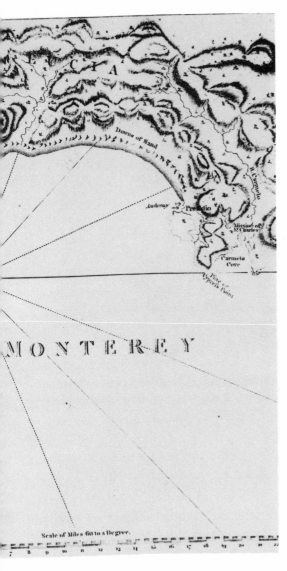

Map (above) of the harbor at Monterey, Alta California, in an English translation of La Perouse's journals. Spain's second Alta California outpost was established here in 1770. The *Santiago*, returning from its arduous northern voyage, put in at Monterey on 29 August 1775.

(From J.F.G. de La Pérouse, *A Voyage Round the World Performed in the Years 1785 . . . 1788 by the Boussole and Astrolabe*, Charts and Plates, 1799. OHS neg #67566)

29

Model of the *Santiago*, from the collections of the Oregon Historical Society. It depicts in miniature Hezeta's flagship, a frigate that was 77 feet along its keel and 27 feet abeam.

(OHS neg.#45008)

Bucareli's choice to lead the expedition was Juan Pérez, a veteran of the Philippine trade prior to his assignment as a pilot at San Blas in 1768. A single vessel, the newly constructed frigate *Santiago* (also called *Nueva Galicia*), was determined to be sufficient to carry out the voyage. The viceroy's instructions to Pérez were elaborate and carefully conceived, leaving little to the imagination as to what was expected of him or how the expedition should proceed.[76] Ostensibly, the purpose of the voyage was to enlarge the King's territories "so that their numerous Indian inhabitants . . . may receive by means of the spiritual conquest the light of the Gospel which will free them from the darkness of idolatry." But Pérez was also given other objectives that probably were of more immediate concern in undertaking the expedition. For one, the *Santiago* was doubling as a supply ship for the settlement at Monterey. Once having accomplished that mission, Pérez was enjoined to sail northward and to specifically make a landing at latitude 60°N. Then, while returning south, Pérez was to follow the coast closely, "never losing sight of it," making landings wherever possible, and recording suitable places for settlement. If foreign settlements were encountered he was to land above them and perform a prescribed formal ceremony of possession-taking. Indian inhabitants were to be treated "affectionately," with no force used against them "except when . . . necessary for self-defense." Finally, Bucareli expected an assessment of the natural resources of the coast.

The *Santiago* sailed out of San Blas in late January 1774, bound for what was supposed to be a brief stop at Monterey to discharge supplies. Instead it was forced to put in at San Diego because of structural troubles with the ship,[77] and by the time the expedition actually cleared Monterey it was well into June. Pérez wisely set a course west by northwest into the Pacific rather than beating north against the coastal winds, and thus he succeeded in making a landfall on the morning of 18 July in the vicinity of latitude 54°N.[78] This was off the northern coast of the Queen Charlotte Islands in present British Columbia, and it was by far the most northerly landfall any Spanish navigator had to date achieved on the west coast of North America. Although friendly contact with the native population was established, no landing was made, and an attempt to push farther north into what was probably Dixon Entrance failed. The expedition turned back on 22 July, considerably below Bucareli's objective of 60°N, and the return voyage down the coast fell even shorter of the viceroy's hopes. A brief stop—but no landing—was made on the coast at latitude 49°30'N (probably Nootka Sound). Later the Olympic Mountains and the central Oregon coast were sighted. But the voyage produced no charts and very little useful information about the coast.

Measured by Bucareli's ambitious objectives, the Pérez voyage would seem to have been a dismal failure. Yet, it had succeeded in finding Drake's secret of gaining high latitudes without beating directly up the coast. Moreover, if one considers that the *Santiago* was sailing without a consort in uncharted waters along a coast frequently shrouded in fog, Pérez's extreme cautiousness may be seen in a more charitable light. Still, the viceroy's eagerness to learn the

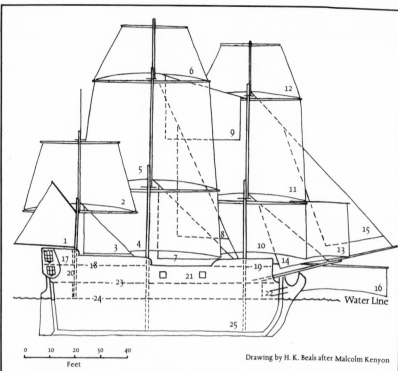

Drawing by H. K. Beals after Malcolm Kenyon

0    10    20    30    40
Feet

## THE FRIGATE SANTIAGO

1. spanker (*mesana*)
2. mizzen topsail (*sobremesana*)
3. mizzen staysail (*vela de estay*)
4. mainsail (*mayor*)
5. main topsail (*gavia*)
6. main-topgallant sail (*juanete mayor*)
7. main staysail (*vela de estay mayor*)
8. main-topmast staysail
   (*vela de estay de gavia*)
9. flying staysail (*vela de estay volante*)
10. foresail (*trinquete*)
11. fore topsail (*velacho*)
12. fore-topgallant sail
    (*juanete de proa*)

13. foresail studding sail
    (*rastrera*)
14. jibsail (*foque*)
15. flying jibsail (*contrafoque*)
16. spritsail (*cebadura*)
17. cabin and topgallant poop
18. quarterdeck
19. forecastle deck
20. berthing
21. waist
22. pantries
23. second deck
24. main deck
25. hold

secrets of the coast that had been briefly glimpsed would require a second expedition.

## THE SECOND BUCARELI EXPEDITION

It was against this background that the expedition of 1775 would be sent forth under the command of first lieutenant of the Royal Navy, Bruno de Hezeta y Dudagoitia. The accompanying translation of its commander's *Diario* records the detailed events of the second voyage of the *Santiago* to the northern coasts, and thus there is no need to repeat them here. But aspects of the expedition concerning its personnel, organization and purposes, deserve some comment as a basis for better understanding the document.

Hezeta arrived in Mexico in late October 1774, accompanied by five other young naval officers sent out from Spain to give the San Blas establishment a full complement of trained leaders. Don Bruno was about 30 years of age at the time of his arrival at San Blas; he had been born about 1744 at Bilbao on the Cantabrian coast of northern Spain.[79] His maternal surname of Dudagoitia is good indication that he was of Basque extraction, and he no doubt grew up in the ancient seafaring traditions of the Bay of Biscay. At age 14, he became a midshipman, initiating a naval career that spanned nearly half a century. In 1784, the Manila galleon, *San Filipe*, sailed under his command,[80] and he was involved in many naval engagements against the French in the mid-1790s as well as later against the English. At the time of his death in 1807, he held the rank of lieutenant general.

Of the five other naval officers who accompanied Hezeta to San Blas in 1774, three would play varying roles in the 1775 expedition. Miguel Manrique would be the central figure in a bizarre incident that happened just as the ships departed San Blas, which resulted in a last-minute shift in command responsibilities affecting two of the other officers in the group: Juan de Ayala would be required to assume Manrique's command, thus placing him in charge of the first Spanish ship fated to enter San Francisco Bay; Juan Francisco de la Bodega y Quadra, in assuming Ayala's command, would be given the opportunity to perform one of the truly epic voyages in the coastal exploration of North America.

33

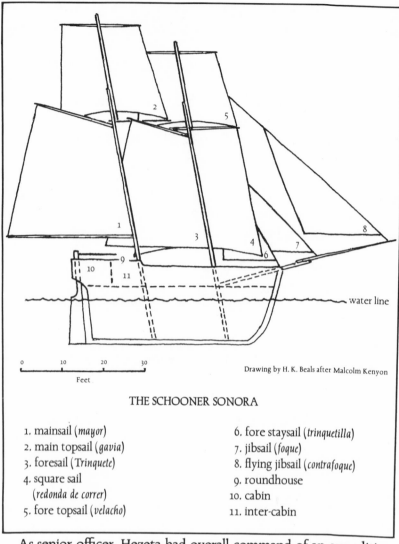

THE SCHOONER SONORA

1. mainsail (*mayor*)
2. main topsail (*gavia*)
3. foresail (*Trinquete*)
4. square sail
   (*redonda de correr*)
5. fore topsail (*velacho*)

6. fore staysail (*trinquetilla*)
7. jibsail (*foque*)
8. flying jibsail (*contrafoque*)
9. roundhouse
10. cabin
11. inter-cabin

As senior officer, Hezeta had overall command of an expedition consisting of three vessels: the flagship *Santiago*; a small escort called *Sonora*, for shallow draft exploring; and a supply ship or packetboat named *San Carlos*.[81] All the ships had been constructed at the San Blas shipyards. The *Santiago* was a three-masted frigate (sp. *fragata*) measuring 77 feet along its keel, and 27 feet abeam. This ship usually is stated to have been about 225-tons, but a study by Malcolm Kenyon of the ships built at San Blas says it "had a burden of 120 Moorsom tons."[82] The *Sonora*, which apparently was officially named *Nuestra Señora de Guadalupe*,[83] was a tiny two-masted schooner (sp.

34

*goleta*) a little under 38 feet long at the keel, and 12.5 feet abeam. Kenyon says its "net tonnage was 31.6 Moorsom tons." The third ship, *San Carlos* (alias *El Toisón*), was a two-masted supply ship (sp. *paquebote*) resembling a brigantine. Its dimensions are given by Kenyon as 64.6 feet along the keel, 23.1 feet abeam, and having a displacement of 195.2 tons.

The personnel of the expedition appear to have numbered nearly 160 officers and men. Juan Pérez returned as second in command of the *Santiago*, with the third officer being a pilot named Cristóbal de Revilla, both of whom are frequently mentioned in the Hezeta *Diario*. As many as 90 men may have been in the *Santiago*'s crew, and as Kenyon observes, "living conditions aboard must have been both crowded and unhealthful."[84] There were also two Franciscan fathers aboard, Fray Miguel de la Campa Cos and Fray Benito de la Sierra, as well as a surgeon named Juan Gonzales.[85] Juan de Ayala began the voyage as captain of the *Sonora*, but, as noted earlier, he was transferred to the *San Carlos*, and Juan Francisco de la Bodega y Quadra assumed command of the little schooner. The *Sonora*'s pilot, Francisco Antonio Mourelle,[86] was thus elevated to second officer, comparable with Pérez's position aboard the frigate. If conditions on the flagship were crowded, the situation on the *Sonora* was anything but spacious, for there were at least 16 men crowded into its cramped quarters.[87] Aboard the *San Carlos*, Ayala was ably assisted by a young pilot named José Cañizares, who later would perform the tasks of charting San Francisco Bay with great distinction. Another Franciscan father, Fray Vicente Santa María, also accompanied the *San Carlos* on its voyage. The packetboat's officers and men probably did not exceed 50; they may have numbered as few as 30, suggesting that conditions aboard it probably were more tolerable than on the other two vessels.[88]

Hezeta seems to have carried basically the same instructions that Bucareli had given Pérez in 1774, although some important modifications were made to adjust them to the circumstances of an expedition now numbering three vessels.[89] The *San Carlos* had orders to proceed alone to Monterey with that settlement's annual provisions; then it was to head northward to locate the entrance of a large estuary or *estero* that had been discovered in 1769 by an overland expedition,[90] and which lay close to Cermeño's Bahía de San Francisco. The *Santiago* and *Sonora* were thus ordered to avoid stop-

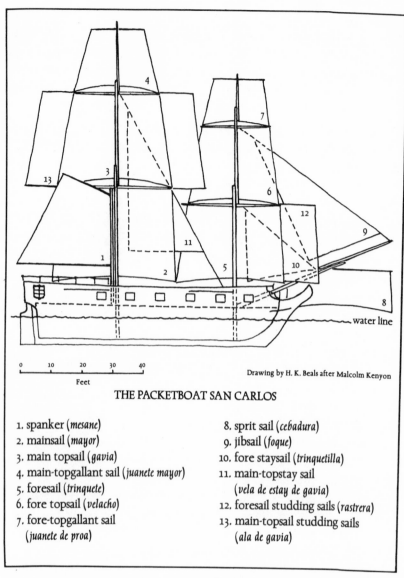

0  10  20  30  40
Feet

Drawing by H. K. Beals after Malcolm Kenyon

## THE PACKETBOAT SAN CARLOS

1. spanker (*mesane*)
2. mainsail (*mayor*)
3. main topsail (*gavia*)
4. main-topgallant sail (*juanete mayor*)
5. foresail (*trinquete*)
6. fore topsail (*velacho*)
7. fore-topgallant sail
   (*juanete de proa*)
8. sprit sail (*cebadura*)
9. jibsail (*foque*)
10. fore staysail (*trinquetilla*)
11. main-topstay sail
    (*vela de estay de gavia*)
12. foresail studding sails (*rastrera*)
13. main-topsail studding sails
    (*ala de gavia*)

ping at Monterey, except in case of emergency, and their mission was to reach latitude 65°N before falling in with the coast. In other respects, Hezeta's instructions governing his return southward along the coast were about the same as those Pérez had been largely unable to fulfill the previous year. Having completed his survey of the northern coasts, Hezeta was also expected to locate and explore the same entrance the *San Carlos* would be searching for at the port of San Francisco.

As Juan Pérez well knew, achieving all these objectives was a tall order, yet the second expedition came as close to doing it as the vagaries of wind, weather and human endurance would permit. On the way up the coast, the *Santiago* and *Sonora* employed the method pioneered by Drake and Pérez of swinging far westward to gain a northing. The conditions met with in 1775, however, were far less favorable than had previously been experienced, and Hezeta was forced to seek the coast prematurely for water and wood. What seemed at first a setback was turned to good advantage by using this as an opportunity to look for a harbor high on the California coast, explore its vicinity, chart it and carry out formal possession-taking ceremonies. This pattern of turning adversity to advantage would be repeated several times, to the expedition's considerable credit.

An uncommonly diverse list of accomplishments would be one of the results of such flexibility in the face of discouraging circumstances. The first European landing north of Cape Blanco (excepting Russian landings in Alaska)—of which there were survivors—occurred on 14 July 1775 on the Olympic Peninsula, mostly as a result of dreadfully poor sailing conditions. While the events of that landing had their tragic aspect, the opportunity was again seized by Hezeta to take formal possession of the land as Bucareli's instructions had required. The little *Sonora*, under Bodega y Quadra, would become separated from the flagship in high seas off Vancouver Island, yet, instead of turning back, the ship pushed on alone with dogged persistence eventually reaching a point off the coast of Chichagof Island in the Alaskan Panhandle in latitude 58°N— within 2° of the goal set for Pérez in 1774.

While the *Santiago* was unable to attain such a high latitude, mainly because of the ravages of scurvy, Hezeta's insistence on following the coast closely on the way south produced the first clear idea of its trends and characteristics. It would also result in two notable geographic discoveries. He found that a great river or strait did indeed lie on this coast, but in the vicinity of latitude 46°N instead of 47° or 43°, and that a prominent cape occupied the shoreline at latitude 43°N, offering the first certainty about a landmark that had hitherto been but vaguely located. The respective

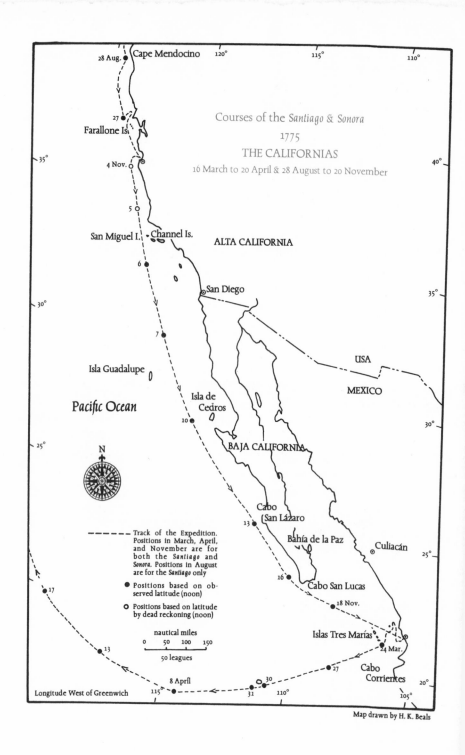

28 Aug. ● Cape Mendocino    120°              115°              110°

27 ●
Farallone Is.

35°                                                                              40°

4 Nov. ○

Courses of the *Santiago* & *Sonora*
1775
THE CALIFORNIAS
16 March to 20 April & 28 August to 20 November

5 ○

San Miguel I. ● Channel Is.          ALTA CALIFORNIA

6 ●

San Diego                                                                        35°

30°

7 ●

Isla Guadalupe  ○

Pacific Ocean                Isla de
                             Cedros
                        10 ●

25°                                                                              30°

N                        BAJA CALIFORNIA

Cabo
(San Lázaro
13 ●
                        Bahía de la Paz        Culiacán
────── Track of the Expedition.        Cabo San Lucas                    25°
        Positions in March, April,
        and November are for
        both the *Santiago* and        16 ●
        *Sonora*. Positions in August
        are for the *Santiago* only            18 Nov. ●
●  Positions based on ob-
   served latitude (noon)
17 ●
○  Positions based on latitude            Islas Tres Marías ●
   by dead reckoning (noon)                                    24 Mar.
        nautical miles                              27 ●        Cabo
13 ●    0    50   100   150                                    Corrientes
            50 leagues                                                      20°
                            8 April  ○ 30
Longitude West of Greenwich  115°      31  110°                105°

Map drawn by H. K. Beals

38

names he bestowed on these features, *Bahía de la Asunción* and *Cabo Diligencias*, have long since passed out of use; but he and the men of the *Santiago* deserve full credit for first locating and charting the Columbia River estuary and fixing Cape Blanco's position. The *San Carlos* crowned these achievements by finding the Golden Gate and making the first maritime entrance into San Francisco Bay,[91] a feat which Hezeta was denied, having to settle instead for an overland trek from Monterey to survey that famous body of water.

Perhaps the expedition could have accomplished more. It did miss a major opportunity in failing to locate the strait at latitude 48° 30' N that subsequently was given Juan de Fuca's name, but so also did James Cook in 1778, as did every other navigator on the coast until the late 1780s. This omission and the failure of the *Santiago* to match the amazing performance of its consort hardly are grounds for one historian to write in the 1840s: "In this expedition, the commander, Heceta, certainly acquired no laurels."[92] By an odd turn of events, the *Diario* of the *Sonora's* second officer, Francisco Mourelle, turned up in London where it was published in an English translation in 1781.[93] The achievements of the schooner were thus well publicized, while those of the flagship remained shrouded for many years in undeserved obscurity. By the time the results of Hezeta's coastal reconnaissance generally became known, others had already received the laurels that had so ungraciously been denied this Biscayan navigator.

## A VICTIM OF OFFICIAL SECRECY?

The failure of the *Santiago's* achievements to receive proper recognition has been attributed in large part to the Spanish government's policy of cloaking such expeditions in a veil of secrecy.[94] While this allegation has merit, Bruno de Hezeta's obscurity may have resulted from chance circumstances conspiring to weave a web of confusion and distortion around the events on the Northwest Coast that summer of 1775.

Word of the two Bucareli expeditions of 1774 and 1775 did in fact leak out at a very early date despite whatever efforts the Spanish government may have exerted to prevent it. Probably the first breach in this official secrecy occurred before either expedition even reached their home port at San Blas in Mexico. On their return voyages south, the vessels of both expeditions stopped over at Monterey, where the Mission of San Carlos Borromeo was located. Among the Franciscan missionaries stationed there was one Fray Francisco Palóu, who had taken upon himself "to note down whatever has happened and may happen . . . in this new vineyard of the Lord."[95] As an eyewitness to the return of both Bucareli expeditions, he naturally recorded the events in some detail. He in fact obtained a copy of the Diario kept by Fray Juan Crespi (one of two chaplains on the 1774 voyage), and he wrote an account of the 1775 voyage that is essentially a summary of the Diario of Fray Miguel de la Campa Cos.

Palóu's history of contemporary events, which would be published as Noticias de la Nueva California, did not appear in print until 1857, but he used materials from his manuscript to write a biography of his missionary colleague, Fray Junípero Serra, which was published in Mexico City in 1787.[96] This biography contains highly condensed but substantially accurate—if fragmentary—accounts of both expeditions.

A second and certainly more serious breach of Spanish security was the unexplained appearance of Mourelle's Diario, translated into English, in a London publication called Miscellanies issued by Daines Barrington six years after the return of the Hezeta-Bodega expedition. Evidence also exists that other information on the Bucareli expeditions must have appeared in English publications before 1778, for James Cook remarked in his journal, while off the Northwest Coast that year, that "some account of the Spaniards having visited this coast was published before I left England."[97] Whatever the source of Cook's earlier information, it was the 1781 appearance of Mourelle's account of the Sonora's role in the 1775 expedition that provided most of what was then known outside Spanish official circles of the voyage. No comparable published sources about the Pérez expedition or the Santiago's role in the Hezeta-Bodega expedition would appear until Palóu's Noticias was published in 1857.

In 1802, geographer Martín Fernández de Navarrete published in Spain an anonymous account of the voyage of two schooners, the Sútil and Mexicana, to the Northwest Coast in 1792, which also included references to both the 1774 and 1775 expeditions.[98] In particular, those references made it clear that the Spanish realized that the *entrada* (or entrance) discovered and called Bahía de la Asunción by Hezeta on 17 August 1775, was the mouth of the same river that Robert Gray had entered in 1792 and named Columbia. Soon thereafter, this matter would become confused, due in part to accounts of the two Bucareli expeditions written by the influential Baron Alexander von Humboldt and published in his *Political Essay on the Kingdom of New Spain*. Humboldt's *Essay*, which appeared in English translation in 1811, says he obtained his information concerning the Pérez voyage "from a manuscript journal, for which I am indebted to the kindness of M. Don Guillermo Aguirre, member of the audiencia of Mexico."[99] This could refer to Pérez' *Diario*, either of the original *Diarios* of the two chaplains on the 1774 voyage, or possibly Palóu's copy of Crespi's account. As a consequence, Humboldt's description of the Pérez expedition is reasonably accurate. His account of the Hezeta-Bodega voyage, however, is quite another matter, for he apparently chose to rely entirely on the Barrington translation of Mourelle's *Diario*, which led him to conclude erroneously that Bodega y Quadra in the *Sonora* had "discovered the mouth of the Rio Columbia, called *entrada de Heceta*."[100] He clearly failed to realize, as also did the translator of Mourelle's account, that after 29 July 1775 the flagship *Santiago* (under Hezeta) and its escort *Sonora* (under Bodega y Quadra) had sailed separate courses, and that their respective discoveries from that point on had been made independently of one another.

Public knowledge of the Bucareli expeditions remained sketchy in the early 19th century probably because there were no urgent reasons to research them beyond the efforts of Humboldt. By the 1840s, however, this began to change as American interest in the Oregon Country intensified. A "Memoir, Historical and Political, on the Northwest Coasts of North America and adjacent Territories" by Robert Greenhow, librarian at the Library of Congress, was communicated to the Senate Select Committee on the Oregon Territory in February 1840, with the purpose of "showing the nature, origin and extent of [the] various claims" to that territory. The "Memoir," as its author later explained, sought "to present a complete, clear, and impartial view of all the discoveries and settlements made or attempted, in those countries by civilized nations . . . from the period when they were first visited by Europeans; founding his statements as much as possible upon original authorities."[101] Four years after the "Memoir" appeared, Greenhow published a book entitled *History of Oregon and California*, expanding his earlier work, and in which was included probably the first English-language account of the Bucareli expeditions drawn from more than a single eyewitness account.

Greenhow obtained from the Depósito Hidrográfico in Madrid copies of the narratives or *Diarios* written by several participants in the expeditions. Concerning the 1774 voyage, these documents included: a narrative written by Pérez for viceroy Bucareli; the *Diario* of Fray Tomás de la Peña; and a statement by second officer Esteban José Martínez. Greenhow believed—whether rightly or not is uncertain—that Humboldt had examined the Crespi *Diario* and he seems to have been content with that, making no attempt to secure a copy of it. He also alludes to the 1802 Navarrete account, believing it to be the earliest Spanish revelation of the voyage,[102] unaware that Palóu's biography of Serra had publicly described the Pérez expedition in 1787 (albeit in Spanish only). As for the Hezeta-Bodega expedition, Greenhow's original sources included: an "official narrative of the whole, drawn up for the viceroy of Mexico"; Bodega y Quadra's *Diario* and "a concise narrative" attributed to him; an extract from Hezeta's *Diario*, "showing his course after his parting with Bodega"; and, of course, the Mourelle *Diario* as translated by Barrington. In addition, he had the Navarrete publication and "various memoirs, reports, correspondence, etc., relative to the northwest coast . . . for the most part, taken directly, or at second hand, from the abstracts of the Journal, given by [C. P. Claret] Fleurieu in his instructions to [Jean François Galaup de] La Pérouse, and his 'Introduction to the Journal of [Étienne] Marchand,' which are filled with errors."[103]

Armed with such a variety of sources, Greenhow thus was able not only to recognize the shortcomings of other secondary accounts, but he could compare and cross-check the eyewitness descriptions for consistency. This resulted in the best understanding up to then of the sequence of events as viewed by various participants. But Greenhow, in undertaking to interpret these events, had difficulty honoring his commitment to impartiality. For example, he remarked concerning the Pérez expedition: "The government of Spain, perhaps acted wisely in concealing the accounts of the expedition, which reflected little honor on the courage or the science of its navigators; but it has thereby deprived itself of the means of establishing beyond question the claim of Pérez to the discovery of the important harbor called *Nootka Sound*, which is now, by general consent, assigned to Captain Cook."[104]

He was, if anything, even less generous about Hezeta's performance in the second expedition. It was Greenhow who wrote: "In this expedition, the commander Heceta, certainly acquired no laurels, though he effected, at least, one discovery [of the Columbia River], from which a nation more enterprising and powerful than Spain might have derived important advantages."[105] Greenhow used every opportunity to insinuate that the commander of the 1775 expedition was always inclined to turn back in the face of adversity. After the expedition was attacked on 14 July by Indians on the central Washington coast, and later when many crewmen were down with scurvy, Hezeta is portrayed as wanting to seize "the opportunity to go back to Monterey."[106] Hezeta's own account—of which Greenhow had only a part—paints an altogether different picture. The only questions at issue, according to the commander, after the Indian attack were whether to seek revenge (which Hezeta opposed) and whether the escort *Sonora* should be sent back to Monterey because of its unseaworthiness (which was decided against). And when the flagship finally did turn back it was, says Hezeta, with great reluctance and only in response to the appeals of Pérez and pilot Cristóbal Revilla on behalf of an ailing crew.

The crediting of Bodega y Quadra with discovery of the Columbia River by so eminent an authority as Alexander von Humboldt and the prejudicial tone of Greenhow's remarks would haunt Don Bruno's reputation as a navigator long after the facts of the 1775 expedition were fully disclosed. Had the Spanish government published a full and authoritative account of the expedition soon after its return, doubtless most of the confusion would have been avoided and the opportunity to twist the facts greatly lessened. The appearance in 1787 of Palóu's published description of the Bucareli expeditions suggests that Spanish officials were either lax in suppressing the release of such news, or what has seemed a concerted policy of official secrecy was really only a lack of appreciation for the importance of information in shaping public opinion. Whatever the truth, whether by accident or design, Spain could have found no more ineffectual means to announce the achievements of her courageous and better-deserving navigators than tucked away in a biography of a then-obscure Franciscan missionary working on the distant edge of civilization.

## THE HEZETA DIARIO

There are two principal manuscript sources for Hezeta's account of the 1775 voyage, both of which are in the Archivo General de la Nación at Mexico City.[107] One version appears to be in the commander's hand, since it bears his signature, while the second is doubtless a duplicate done by a copyist. The Archivo General de Indias at Sevilla also possesses a third manuscript version of the text that is a certified copy.[108] Microfilm versions of these documents, in the manuscript collection of the Oregon Historical Society, were used in making the accompanying translation.

Two extracts from Hezeta's *Diario* have been previously published in English translations. These include the entries relating to the discovery of the Columbia River and the description of the expedition's stay at Trinidad Harbor. Greenhow says he secured a certified copy of an "Extract from the Report of Captain Bruno Heceta . . . preserved in the Hydrographic Office at Madrid," covering the period of 17 to 18 August.[109] From this, the Spanish text and an English translation were printed in his *History of Oregon and California* (pp. 430–33, 4th ed.) which first appeared in 1844 at Boston. No translator's name is given (Another translation of Hezeta's entry for 17 August, made by Charles Walters, appears in a book published in 1976 entitled *The Chinook Indians: Traders of the Lower Columbia River* (pp. 31–32), by Robert H. Ruby and John A. Brown). The second extract to be published in English from the *Diario* appeared in 1952 in a book entitled *The Four Ages of Tsurai* (pp. 29–44), by Robert Heizer and John Mills. The translation, made by Donald Cutter, covers the period 9 to 19 June, when the expedition was among the Yurok Indians at Trinidad Harbor.

Hezeta's *Diario* records the events of an exploring mission of great significance in the early European penetration of the Pacific Northwest, written from the commander's perspective. Yet, no full-length English translation of it has appeared. Both of the chaplains aboard the *Santiago* kept diaries, which have been translated

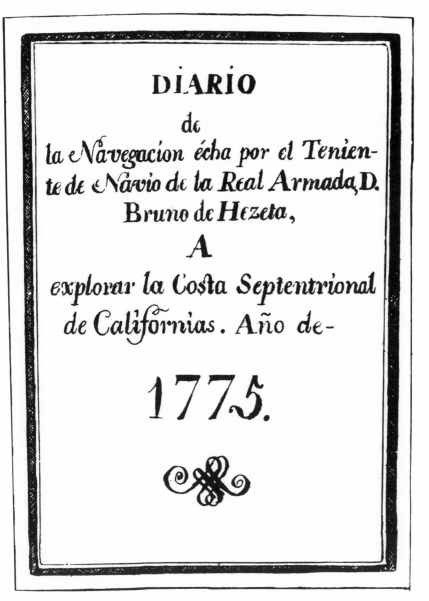

# DIARIO

de

la Navegacion écha por el Teniente de Návio de la Real Armada, D.
Bruno de Hezeta,

A

explorar la Costa Septentrional
de Californias. Año de-

# 1775.

Title page of Hezeta's *Diario*, from the version that appears to have been copied from the original.
(Archivo General de la Nación, Mexico City. OHS neg.#67565)

Diario de la navegazion que deve hacer con el Divino Auxi-
lio el Teniente de Navio D.n Bruno de Hezeta en la Fraga.ta de
su mando S.n Iago (alias) nueba Galicia, y en conserva de la
Goleta Sonora que esta a su orn y se dirigen a los descubrim.to
de las costas Septentrionales de la California deve el departamento de S.n Blas situado en la latt.d de 21 g.s y 30 minu.s N. y
Long.d Occidental de Paris 110 g.s segun la Carta de M. Bellin
que es por la que se ha dirigido.

### Advertencias

La tabla que se pone al fin de este diario esta sujeta al termi-
no meaie de los diarios en ella se insertan cuantas noticias pue-
den contribuir al conocim.to de Vientos mares y corrientes para Go-
vernarse en lo succesibo en estas Navegaziones.

La Long.d se expresa por la diferencia que ai desde S.n
Blas a la situazion en que se halla la Frag.ta y asi el Lector q.e
quisiere Calcular la que tiene respecto al meridiano de Thenerif
Paris y otro contando segun costumbre antigua toda la circun-
ferencia de Orive de oriente a Poniente substraera de la Long.d se
S.n Blas la candidad de g.s que expresa este diario, Occidentales.

### Dia 16 al 17 de Marzo de 1775.

A las 4 de la tarde se concluio la rebista de Pagam.to de las tri-
pulaziones de este buque y Goleta Sonora a las 10 de la noche
empese a Zarpar con venlolina Terral a las 11 concluida esta
faena ize fuerza de vela en V.ta del O acompañado del Paquebot
S.n Carlos y Goleta a las 7 ¼ de la mañana ynaie por esperar
a esta que se hallaba atrasada como dos leg.s y aviendole cal-
mado el V.to se vio en la preficion de anclar a la misma dis-
tancia de este Buque por que las corrientes rechazaban su in-
tento a las 9 de la m.a meti la lancha dentro demorandome S.n
Blas al E dist.a 0 leg.s

### Dia 17 al 18

A la 1 de la tarde haviendo refrescado la virsa por el NO y con-

Initial page of Hezeta's *Diario* text, from the version that appears to
be in the commander's own hand.
(Archivo General de la Nación, Mexico City. OHS neg.#68532)

and published,[110] and hence their views and descriptions of events are those most often cited.

The translation that follows is offered in the hope that a broader understanding of this remarkable expedition will emerge from having Hezeta's own account of the voyage available in English.

# FOR HONOR AND COUNTRY
## THE DIARY

The Spanish royal coat-of-arms (previous page) as depicted on coins issued at Spanish American mints in the 18th century.

# Diary

OF

# the Voyage made by First Lieutenant of the Royal Navy, Don Bruno de Hezeta,

TO

# Explore the Northern Coast of California in the Year 1775

D iary of the voyage that is the duty of first lieutenant Bruno de Hezeta to perform, with divine assistance, in the frigate under his command *Santiago* (also called *Nueva Galicia*), escorted by the schooner *Sonora*, which is at his service; being sent out to make discoveries on the northern coasts of California from the Department of San Blas, situated in latitude 21 degrees, 30 minutes N. and longitude West of Paris 110 degrees, according to M. Bellin's map, used by them for directions.

*Foreword*

The table put at the end of this diary is based upon the average of the diaries included. Whatever information the table can contribute to the knowledge of winds, tides and currents is for governing successive such voyages.

Longitude is expressed in terms of the difference between San Blas and the position of the frigate, and thus the reader who wants to calculate the frigate's longitude with respect to the meridian of Tenerife, Paris or some other place, reckoned by ancient custom, anywhere on the circumference of the earth from east to west, will subtract from the longitude of San Blas the amount of degrees west expressed in this diary.[1]

*16th to 17th March 1775*

At four in the afternoon, review of the payment of the crews of this ship and the schooner *Sonora* was finished. At ten in the evening, I commenced to weigh anchor with a breeze off the land. At eleven, having finished this task, I set sail on a course W., accompanied by the packetboat *San Carlos* and the schooner. At seven-thirty in the morning I cast anchor to wait for the schooner, which was found to be lagging behind some two leagues. The wind having fallen calm, it found it necessary to anchor at exactly the same distance from this ship because the currents had frustrated its intentions. At nine in the morning I put the launch in. San Blas lies toward the E. a distance of 3 leagues.

17th to 18th

At one in the afternoon, the breeze having freshened from the NW, I realized it was impossible for the schooner to stay in company with us. I set sail, and stationed myself in its immediate vicinity. The distance to San Blas is 2 leagues. At ten in the evening, with a breeze off the land, I signaled to make sail. I gave orders to sail W, and setting my sails in accordance with the slight headway of my escort, I arrived at noon where I fixed the distance to San Blas at 5 leagues, bearing WSW.[2]

18th to 19th

At one-thirty in the afternoon I anchored at the distance and direction from San Blas cited above, influenced by the wind having moved to the NE. At two-thirty in the afternoon I got the schooner into my immediate vicinity. At three, I was passed by the packet-boat *San Carlos* (which had imitated my maneuvers up to then) heading on the leeward side back toward the land. At five, I anchored a distance of two leagues from the latter ship. At five-thirty it discharged two cannons, raising a red flag to the top of the main mast. In view of this demonstration the launch was sent out, and at nine-thirty in the evening it returned with the commander [of the ship] mentioned above. It was clear from the first statements he made that he was incoherent.[3] This unfortunate loss of his faculties, compelled me to resolve, with agreement among the officers, to replace the *San Carlos'* commander with second lieutenant Don Juan de Ayala, commander of the schooner *Sonora*, and to have the latter responsibility taken over by Don Juan de Bodega y Quadra who is of the same rank and second in command on the schooner, continuing his merit. I had the ill Don Miguel Manrique returned in the launch to San Blas, in order for him to recover his health.

19th to 20th

At seven in the morning, I made sail, turning to a course SSW. At twelve-thirty, the distance E to San Blas was fixed at five leagues.

52

At one in the afternoon, recognizing by a sighting taken of the land that the current was pushing us off course, I anchored in nine *brazas*. At two-thirty in the morning, accompanied by the escort, I set sail and steered to the W with the wind out of the S. At noon the latitude was observed to be 21°39′.

*21st to 22nd*

I continued on the same course with the same wind. At two in the afternoon the launch of the packetboat *San Carlos* arrived at this ship. Its commander notified me in writing that he was carrying on deck various cases and bundles which greatly served to inconvenience the crew, risking the ship in case of a storm. To this, I responded for him to attempt to transfer them at the first opportunity. At four-thirty in the afternoon I anchored in six-and-one-half *brazas*, sighting Piedra Blanca, bearing SSE 5°S; [Isla] Isabela was to the W.[4] I corrected the compass variation of 5 1/4 degrees. At seven in the evening they transferred the bundles, and deposited them in the ship's hold. At ten in the evening I made sail, towing the schooner, steering on a course to the W with a little wind to the landward. As the sun came up, I sighted [Isla] Isabela bearing to the SW a distance of three leagues. I reckoned the latitude at N 21°49′.

*22nd to 23rd*

At twelve-thirty I veered to a course heading SE, with a fresh wind out of the NNW blowing steadily always. At four in the afternoon, I lowered the foretopmast because of a split, about which I had information from the previous voyage [in 1774], and I held it in reserve only in case of emergency. In view of this damage and finding the wind fresh out of the WNW, I anchored at four-thirty in eight *brazas*.

A Spanish map of 1778 (following pages) depicting the waters Hezeta traversed between San Blas and Isla Socorro. The legend reads:
Map comprising the navigation from the port of San Blas to *Roca partida* [cleft rock], with the other islands encompassed in this distance, which are located according to the various surveys, bearings and solar observations made of their latitudes by the pilots of His Majesty's packetboat *San Carlos*, on the voyage made to the port of San Diego in the year 1778.
(OHS neg.#68560)

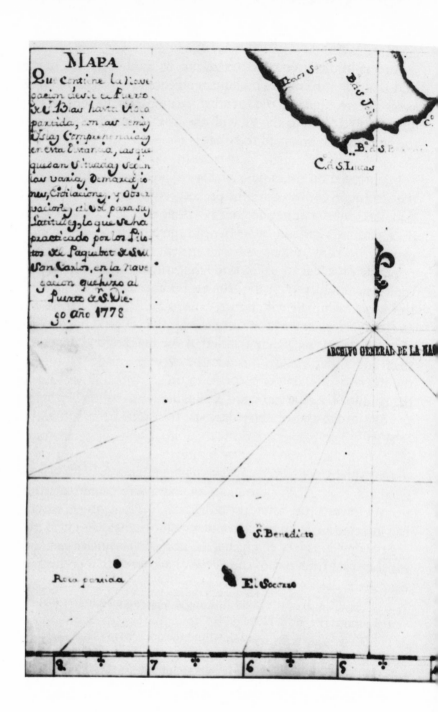

**MAPA**

Que contiene la Nave
gacion desde el Puerto
del Blas hasta Vela
partida, con las demas
Islas Comprehendidas
en esta Carta, las que
quedan situadas segun
las varias Demarcacio
nes, Estivaciones, y Obser
vacion, &.c. para su
Latitudes, lo que se ha
practicado por los Pilo
tos del Paquebot de Su
Don Carlos, en la nave
gacion que hizo al
Puerto de S. Die
go año 1778

C. d S. Lucas

B. d S. B

Pan S

Bas Jo

c°

S. Benedicto

El Socorro

Roca partida

8       7       6       5

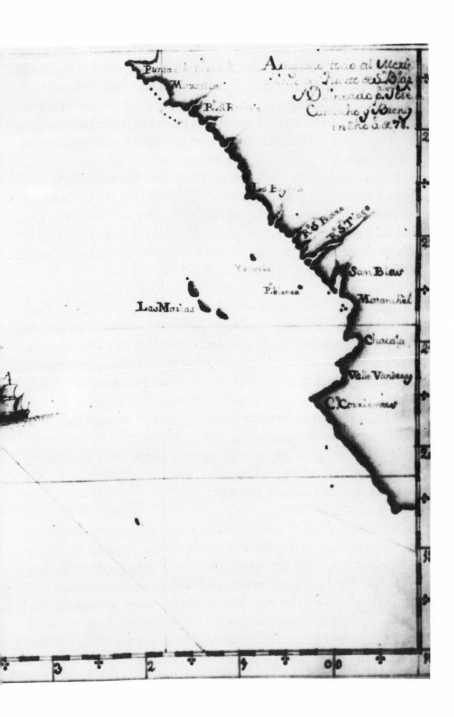

Punta del ...
Mazatlan
R. de R...

A... todo al Mexi...
... a ... de Dia...
Delineado p. Jose
Car... cho y Bren...
en ... de 78.

La B... a

R. de B...
R. S.T...

Y...ela

San Blas

P. blanca

Matanchel

Las Moitas

Chacala

Valle Vanderg

C. Corrientes

3    2

55

[Isla] Isabela is four leagues distant bearing WNW 5°E. Work proceeded without letup to put in place a wooden reinforcing sleeve with two lanyards on the foremast.[5] The task was concluded at three in the morning. I made sail with a wind out of the NNE with the schooner in tow, and steered to the W. I observed the latitude at 21°48', with [Isla] Isabela bearing NNE a distance of two leagues.

### 23rd to 24th

I continued to steer the same course. As the sun went down, the SE island of the Marías bore S 1/4 SW, distance three leagues.[6] At one-thirty at night, with a north wind, I steered to the S intending to pass leeward of this island. At noon, it was reckoned at NNW, one-half league distant, and I observed the latitude to be 21°13' N, and the longitude west of San Blas at 1°20'.

### Notes

I ran before the wind in order to pass leeward of the [Islas] Marías, contrary to the customary sailing of the ships of the Department of San Blas, because it made no difference to me to go up a degree having so many to gain anyway in the assigned mission; and also because it relieved the crew from the weariness of the troublesome task of repeatedly anchoring and weighing anchor, which is necessary to gain the windward side of these islands. I can assure you that this decision has been advantageous to me, since I have avoided the delays that regularly happen, and I have taken advantage of this to gain longitude, which was facilitated by the favorable winds for going upward.

The 29th day of March I came upon the Isla de Socorro, so called by some, or by others, Santo Tomás.[7] I was held up until the 4th of April, powerless to lose sight of it. The continual calms made the effects—I mean the efforts—I made to separate myself from it futile. On this same day the horizon began to darken so much that only at midday did the sun allow itself to be seen somewhat. The name of this island could be doubted if it were not known that in the time when Hernando Grijalva sailed no foreigner had visited these waters.[8] Declaring it to be the same island, according to the course and distance he sailed after his departure from Tehauntepec in the year 1524, I will call it from now on Santo Tomás which is the same name its discoverer gave it.

This island stretches NW by SE about 5 leagues and is three leagues wide. The cape on the NW terminates in low land with some small islets, and on the SE in a craggy coast. In the center is a peak which can be seen from afar. The swirling currents are so rapid in its vicinity that on the night of 3 April they impeded the steering of this ship, causing me to veer into the wind several times. Notwithstanding a calm wind favorable to us, on one of these sudden turns I could not avoid colliding with the schooner (which was always in tow). There was no damage as a result of it.

This delay gave me an opportunity to confirm the manifest barrenness of the place. I was unable to discover a tree, vegetation, or watering place on a shore with an anchorage, even though I tried to do so, nor was I able to replenish my water supply.

According to my observations, I calculated the middle of this island to be in latitude 18°50' N., and longitude west of San Blas 5°30'.

From this longitude the qualities of the climate began to diversify. The winds were cooler and less humid. The seas were more disturbed by the winds of the first [NE] quadrant; and the seas set themselves against those of the fourth [NW quadrant], which generally always persist, not permitting the frigate and the schooner to make progress in proportion to their efforts under sail. The currents, which up to now had caused me to turn down to the south, became less violent and somewhat different.

The birds, called *centenares* and *vavijunces*, allowed themselves to be seen nearly every day up to the end of April.[9] Various kinds of fish also accompanied us up to the middle of this month, whereupon the winds began to blow from the first [NE] quadrant.

On the 21st day of May I resolved to call a meeting to take opinions about heading for land which we were obliged to do because our water supply was running low. The sailors were already tired of suffering from the small amount of water they were given. They needed the relief which I wanted to give them, because I consid-

Jacques Bellin's *Carte Reduite de L'Ocean Septentrional* [small-scale map of the northern ocean] (following pages) published in 1766 by the French Dépot de la Marine. It shows the 1741 voyages and discoveries of Bering and Chirikov, but otherwise its depiction of the Northwest Coast is mostly speculative. Hezeta says he carried a copy of this map aboard the *Santiago*, referring to it as the expedition's principal cartographic guide.

(Wagner Collection, Honnold Library, Claremont Colleges, Los Angeles)

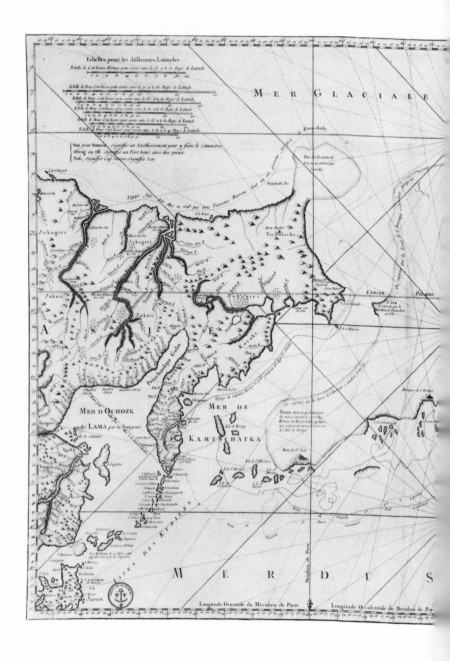

Echelles pour les differentes Latitudes

Echelle de Cent Lieues Marines pour servir entre le 76. et le 70. Degré de Latitude

Echelle de Deux Cent Lieues pour servir entre le 70. et le 66. Degré de Latitude
Echelle de Deux Cent Lieues pour servir entre les 66. et le 60. Degré de Latitude
Echelle de Deux Cent Lieues pour servir entre le 60. et le 55. Degré de Latitude
Echelle de Deux Cent Lieues pour servir entre le 55. et le 50. Degré de Latitude
Echelle de Deux Cent Lieues pour servir entre le 50. et le 45. Degré de Latitude

Sun pour Simovie, signifie un Etablissement pour y faire le Commerce
Ostrog, ou Ost, signifie un Fort bâti avec des pieux.
Noss, signifie Cap Oзero signifie Lac.

MER GLACIALE

Kamtschatka

CERCLE POLAIRE

JUKAGIRI

ASIE

MER D'OCHOZK
appellé LAMA par les Toungouses

MER DE KAMTSCHATKA

MER DU S

Longitude Orientale du Meridien de Paris    Longitude Occidentale du Meridien de Paris

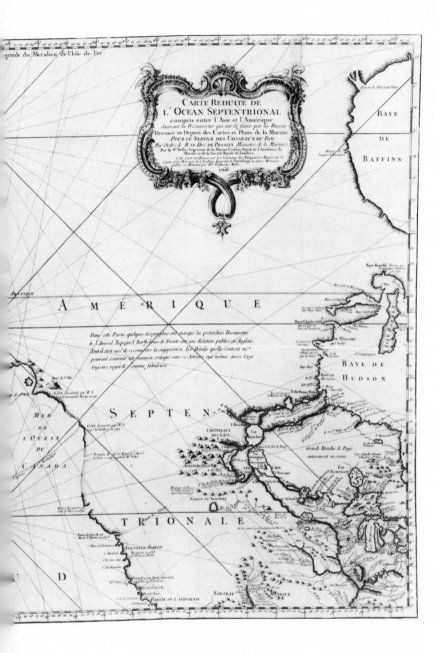

CARTE REDUITE DE
L'OCEAN SEPTENTRIONAL
compris entre l'Asie et l'Amerique
Suivant les Decouvertes qui ont été faites par les Russes
Dressée au Depost des Cartes et Plans de la Marine
POUR LE SERVICE DES VAISSEAUX DU ROY
Par Ordre de M LE DUC DE PRASLIN Ministre de la Marine
Par le S.r Bellin Ingenieur de la Marine Censeur Royal de l'Academie du
Marine et de la Societé Royale de Londres
1766

BAYE
DE
BAFFINS

A M E R I Q U E

S E P T E N -

- T R I O N A L E

BAYE DE
HUDSON

MER
DE
L'OUEST
DU
CANADA

59

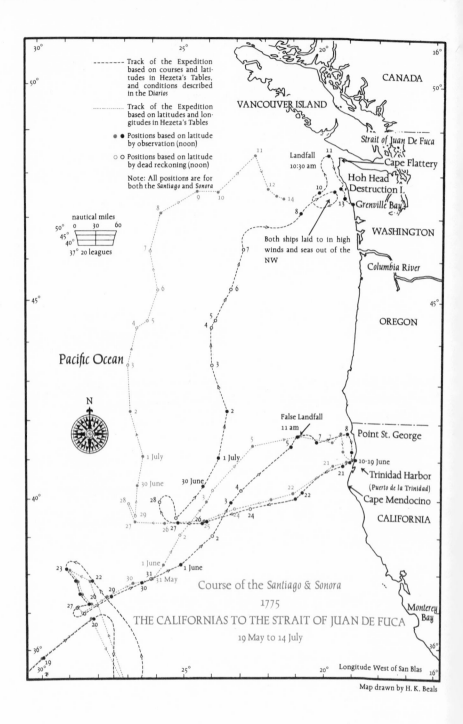

Track of the Expedition based on courses and latitudes in Hezeta's Tables, and conditions described in the *Diarios*

Track of the Expedition based on latitudes and longitudes in Hezeta's Tables

● ● Positions based on latitude by observation (noon)

○ ○ Positions based on latitude by dead reckoning (noon)

Note: All positions are for both the *Santiago* and *Sonora*

nautical miles
50° 0    30    60
45°
40°
37° 20 leagues

30°                25°                        20°                16°

CANADA

VANCOUVER ISLAND

Strait of Juan De Fuca

Landfall
10:30 am

Cape Flattery

Hoh Head

Destruction I.

Grenville Bay

Both ships laid to in high winds and seas out of the NW

WASHINGTON

Columbia River

OREGON

*Pacific Ocean*

N

False Landfall
11 am

Point St. George

10-19 June

Trinidad Harbor
(*Puerto de la Trinidad*)

Cape Mendocino

CALIFORNIA

1 July

30 June

1 June

31 May

Monterey Bay

Course of the *Santiago* & *Sonora*

1775

THE CALIFORNIAS TO THE STRAIT OF JUAN DE FUCA

19 May to 14 July

36°

30° 19                25°                        20°     Longitude West of San Blas     16°

Map drawn by H. K. Beals

60

ered them extremely fatigued. The judgment of Don Francisco de Bodega y Quadra and pilot Don Francisco Maurelle was to continue up to the Río Aguilar located on the map in 43°,[10] while that of Don Juan Pérez and Don Cristóbal Revilla was to head for Monterey. My determination was to go with the first opinion because such a landfall that high had the potential of discovering some port (which proved true) and, in any case, we would easily have the refuge of Monterey in case of emergency to replenish what we lacked.

On the 1st of June the winds began to blow from the third [SW] quadrant, got stronger, freshening in proportion to the waxing of the moon, and carried us to within sight of land.

### 6th to 7th

At eleven in the morning land was descried, but the fog was so thick it caused me to doubt the sighting.

### 7th to 8th

I continued to press on, turning to the NE. Being now very close to land, within four leagues, I assured myself it was in fact land. I sighted what appeared to be capes, but I was mistaken in no small way. Calm weather all night and violent currents moving to the S caused me to lose latitude. At dawn, I found myself seemingly in an inlet, formed in the clouds, looking like a mountainous and snowy coast so similar to what is represented on the maps of M. Bellin,[11] printed in the year 1766, based on information from the Imperial Academy of Petersburg, in that latitude, that the least credulous person would have said the same.

### 8th and 9th

The desire to find some port in order to refresh my crews, even with the horizon jet black, obliged me to follow a NE course. With the NW wind the sky cleared, and I realized that the coast runs along in the form of an imperceptible curve. Although I continued to approach closer, all that came into view were some small inlets, unsheltered from the wind and sea, in which to run.[12] I tacked at nightfall, turning outward, and lay to, tacking again at two in the morning. I drew to within a distance of one league from the coast, and at ten-thirty I recognized that this part of the coast showed no sign of offering safety for these ships, and ran before the wind to the S. Even with a heavy sea running, I continued in the same close proximity to the land so that the smallest harbor would not be hidden from me. The coast being sown with little islets or offshore rocks made me suspicious of the evenness of the bottom, compelling me to take precautions to send the schooner out ahead of me. It was in this way that I secured complete success, because of the intelligence and devotion shown during the cruise by the schooner's commander, Don Juan Francisco de Bodega y Quadra, and his pilot Don Francisco Maurelle. Not only have they been on the lookout for the most favorable sea for me to perform this dangerous maneuver, but they also contributed by carrying the greatest press of sail I have ever seen up to now, minimizing the very poor sailing qualities of the ship under his charge. Through his zealous vigilance he has avoided being swamped by the numerous heavy seas, currents and winds the two ships have frequently been subjected to, and which required of them, on such an extended voyage, the trouble of sailing in tow. I also cannot leave unexpressed the same contribution in this matter by this ship's second officer, Don Juan Pérez, and the pilot, Don Francisco Revilla,[13] who, along with the crews, tirelessly performed the consequential maneuvers, showing nothing but a desire to sacrifice themselves for the service.

### 9th

I continued exploring the coast following the same course. At one-thirty, I sighted three canoes of Indians who were diligently attempting to approach this ship. I shortened sail and they arrived, all naked and with their hair in disarray. In a short time they had exchanged with the sailors hide clothing that they had carried hidden. In a little while they pushed off and followed our course into the harbor, where I anchored at 3:30 in the afternoon shortly after the schooner. I proceeded to sound an enclosed port formed by a small peninsula into which I determined to warp.[14] This task was finished on the following day at two in the morning, finding ourselves anchored in three-and-one-half to four *brazas* aft and four *brazas* forward.

### 10th

In the afternoon, I went ashore with the officers and some armed men in order to see if the show of friendship by the Indians on the previous day, when they visited this ship, was as real as that shown when I visited them on the beach in the company of Don Juan Francisco de la Bodega y Quadra and Don Francisco Maurelle. During the visit, we expressed our well wishes by presenting them various bead trinkets, part of which I had received from his Majesty's account, while others were brought on his own by the above-mentioned Don Francisco for the same purpose. I noticed that they were somewhat suspicious that afternoon, although they made no attempt to interfere with us. I returned on board before it grew dark, after my crew had thoroughly mingled with them.

11th

I determined to take possession on this day for it is the day honoring the Most Holy Trinity. At dawn I sent out Don Cristóbal de Revilla with a number of armed men to find the trails that connect the mainland to the peninsula that forms this harbor, and to set up a chapel where the first mass was to be celebrated with as much ceremony as possible. Complete freedom was assured the measures taken to facilitate the divine worship, since the Indians of this vicinity never thought of interfering, although in coming down the men were accompanied by some of the Indians from the nearby rancherías.[15] In company with the commander of the schooner, the reverend fathers, officers, and armed men of both ships, I fixed the cross on the beach, and, formed up in military order, we recited the first adoration. Afterward, we continued on the way up to the top in the most orderly fashion that the narrow trails would permit, where the chapel had been prepared, and took possession without omitting the most meticulous formalities stated in my Instructions. The mass was celebrated and the Reverend Father Fray Miguel de la Campa delivered a sermon. These proceedings were solemnized by several volleys of gunfire. We returned to our assigned ships which, with banners flying, saluted with three volleys of artillery and "Long Live the King." In the afternoon I went to the ranchería where I found them overcome with fear, but as we continued to give them presents they cast their fear aside and clearly demonstrated to me their desire to establish perpetual friendship with us. I assured them of such friendship as long as they maintained the cross which had been set up this morning. After pointing out to them why the situation warrants this, they all offered to do so.[16]

12th

I sent part of the crew to get water and wood accompanied by some armed men who remained idle because of the good relations with the Indians. This contributed much to making the task easier since it was troublesome to maintain them under arms. Additional replenishment is found in abundance on the beach closest to the anchorage, a distance of a musket shot from the ships.

### 13th

During my stay in this port I observed through careful investigation that the daily tides ebbed only 3 1/2 Parisian feet. I secured the ship under my charge in sufficient water for it to ride in six [*brazas?*] at low tide, allowing for pitching of the ship. At three in the morning the rudder touched bottom, and I withdrew a little, anchoring in four *brazas* aft. I continued to re-provision, the same as on the previous day, and to cut a pole for the foretopmast after finding the two I had were nearly useless. I will leave until some other occasion to describe the good quality of this location for replenishing shortages of this kind, as well as for taking on water.

### 14th

The entire day was occupied in working on the mast, ballasting the ship and taking on water and wood. At review that night it was noticed that two apprentice seamen, José Antonio Rodrigues and Pedro Lorenzo, were missing.

### 15th

I armed some men this morning and in their company went to the *ranchería* with the purpose of investigating the whereabouts of the deserters. The nervousness of the Indians made me think they were guilty, and I took into custody the captain of this *ranchería* and one from another who happened to be there, both of whom, with considerable urging, came along after a short while. Although still preoccupied by the same unsubstantiated suspicion, I relented and returned them ashore, giving them presents on the advice of Don Juan Francisco la Quadra and the reverend fathers.

### 16th

The work of taking on water, wood and ballast went ahead with the same effort, this being the first stopover in which I had resupplied. The apprentice seaman, Pedro Lorenzo, one of the deserters I mentioned yesterday, returned, and a statement was taken from him. He said: "The chief of the Indian *ranchería* suggested that I stay in their company, offering dominion of all those lands with whatever resources were needed for sustenance. Having decided to remain, I was led off by the Indians, provided with food and taken under guard to a tree-covered summit immediately overlooking the anchorage." But the guards who accompanied him became careless and, repenting his crime, he determined to escape, which he in fact did. With my first suspicions thus confirmed, I spent time this afternoon with some of the people thinking they would return the other deserter to me at the first threats. Paralyzed with fear, they offered apologies in great confusion. I made the informer [Lorenzo] come, and in their presence he stated that the confession he had made this morning was false. I punished this individual on the spot, satisfying the Indians, who throughout the length of my stay continued the same expressions of true friendship.[17]

### 17th

I continued outfitting for departure, sparing no effort to speed the preparation along, and I put the pickets [guards] out to draw a map geometrically.

### 18th

On this day the map of the port was finished, having been drawn up in collaboration with the captain of the schooner, Don Juan Francisco de la Quadra, and the first pilot, Don Francisco Maurelle. I went in company with the latter to explore a river, which was given the name *Tórtolas* [turtledoves],[18] and to examine

---

The first map of Trinidad Harbor on the northern California coast (following pages). Hezeta called it *Puerto de la Trinidad*, and there the expedition remained for ten days from 9 to 19 June. Trinidad Head is at A, where religious services were held and a cross erected. The ships anchored in the cove at B. The location of the nearby village of Tsurai is shown at C. The place Hezeta called *Cañada* is marked D at the extreme southeast corner of the map.

The map's inscription reads:

Map of the port of Trinidad situated below 40[°] 07['], latitude, and in longitude west of San Blas 19[°] 04['], discovered and charted by the commander of this expedition, first lieutenant Don Bruno de [H]ezeta y Dudagoitia, second lieutenant Don Juan Francisco de la Bodega y Quadra, and the pilot Don Francisco Maurelle, on the voyage of discoveries they made on the northern coasts of California by order of His Excellency, Frey Don Antonio Bucareli y Ursúa, Viceroy of New Spain, in the year 1775.

A. Mount of the cross    C. Indian *ranchería*
B. Anchorage             D. Ravine

(Archivo General de Indias, Sevilla. From photograph in The Bancroft Library)

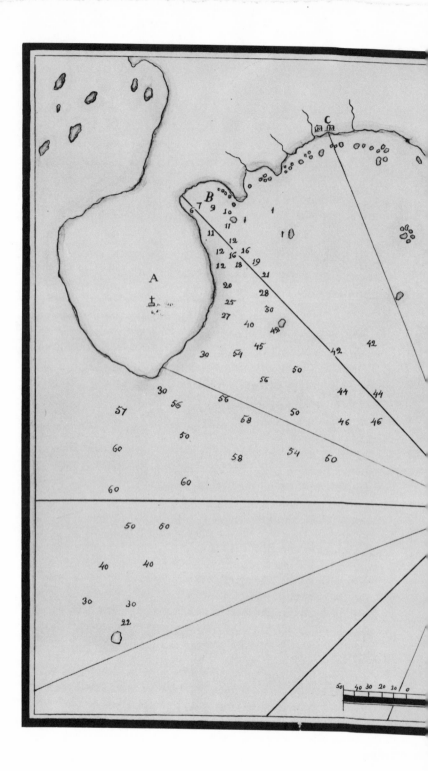

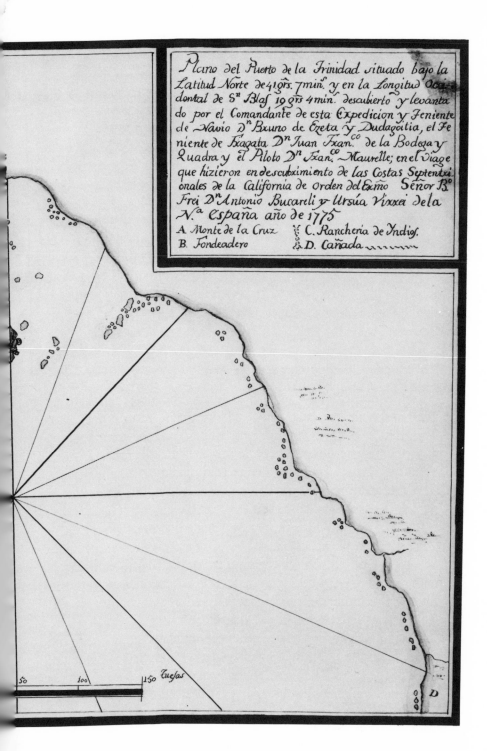

*Plano del Puerto de la Trinidad situado bajo la Latitud Norte de 41 grs. 7 min. y en la Longitud Occidental de Sn. Blas 19 grs. 4 min. descubierto y levantado por el Comandante de esta Expedicion y Teniente de Navio Dn Bruno de Ezeta y Dudagoitia, el Teniente de Fragata Dn Juan Franco de la Bodega y Quadra y el Piloto Dn Franco Maurelle; en el viage que hizieron en descubximiento de las Costas Septentrionales de la California de orden del Exmo Señor Bo Frei Dn Antonio Bucareli y Ursúa Virrei de la Na España año de 1775*

*A. Monte de la Cruz*   *C. Rancheria de Yndios.*
*B. Fondeadero*   *D. Cañada*

50   100   150   Tuesas

D

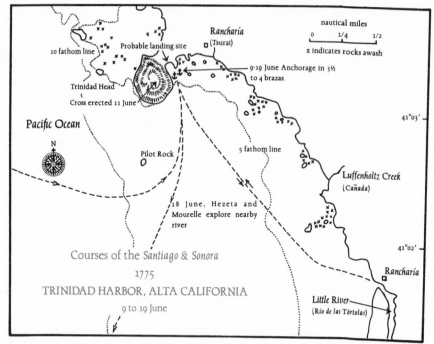

Labels within the map:

nautical miles
0    1/4    1/2
x indicates rocks awash

Ranchería
(Tsurai)

Probable landing site
10 fathom line

9-19 June Anchorage in 3½
to 4 brazas

Trinidad Head
Cross erected 11 June

41°03'

Pacific Ocean

N

Pilot Rock

5 fathom line

Luffenholtz Creek
(Cañada)

18 June, Hezeta and
Mourelle explore nearby
river

41°02'

Courses of the *Santiago* & *Sonora*
1775
TRINIDAD HARBOR, ALTA CALIFORNIA
9 to 19 June

Ranchería

Little River
(Río de las Tórtolas)

its adjacent fields, forests and so forth. The nearby Indians extended the greatest hospitality, and, wanting to return their favors, I took most of them on board my launch to repay their good behavior with glass beads. I went down to the nearby *rancheria* where, with melancholy faces, they were told of the departure that was about to take place. I gave them presents, offering to return, at which they showed satisfaction.[19]

During my stay in this port of Trinidad, although occupied in discharging my responsibilities, I was not prevented from taking some time off to observe the customs of the Indians of this small village, and its neighbors who frequently got together to visit us, as well as to examine the advantages offered by this country for agriculture and settlement, in case that is considered.

The physiognomy of these and neighboring Indians is one of medium plumpness, robustness and agility, without beauty among either of the sexes. They are dark complexioned, with long, straight hair, and twinkling black eyes; they are beardless. The men wear no clothing even to cover their private parts, and only when they are forced by the cold do they cover themselves with the well-tanned hides of deer, bison, antelope, bear, or sea otter, and some sort of cloaks woven from rabbit skins and such other skins flexible enough to permit their use without discomfort.[20]

The women cover themselves from the waist to the knees with skirts of hide or grass, some of which are finished off in different threads as a fringe, and in others they begin and end [in a fringe]. Thus, carefully worn, these preserve the modesty that is appropriate to their nature. Concerned with personal adornment, like their sex everywhere, they are eager for glass beads; but most of them have no great appreciation for flannels and woolens.

The captains and their sons, on special days, wear on their heads a garland of fine hides, grasses, or feathers, which distinguishes them from the rest.

These Indians are of a peaceable temperament, docile and timid; they love, revere and obey the eldest, who governs with his councils. Based on my information, each *rancheria* is made up of only the descendants of these elders. When old age renders a captain useless for war, the son most qualified becomes captain.

My lack of understanding of minerals kept me from searching for them; but, having entrusted this concern to two members of the crew who were considered knowledgeable, I was informed that in the small area they explored they had seen nothing that promised such a discovery.

Iron is the metal they [the Indians] hold in particular esteem because they know about its advantages in the use of weapons. The weapons they use are the arrow, lance, knife or dagger, whose points or sharp edges are of well-worked flint. They also use iron knives, which generally are carried dangling from the neck on a cord, and which they hold grasped in the hand when they are apprehensive.

With the utmost curiosity, I inquired on several occasions as to where those iron knives had come from or with whom they had bartered for them. They all responded unanimously by pointing to the coast toward the north, except for one who, with lively and intelligible signs, suggested to us that his had been made from a spike, which came from the fragment of a ship the sea had cast on the beach.[21]

When they go to war or deal with enemies, they paint their face and body black and other colors, no doubt believing it makes them more horrible and fearsome.

They say unequivocally that they have seen no ship in these waters, but they have information that ships frequent the coast, pointing to the south. My opinion is that they are those that come from Monterey.

These Indians are engaged in a well-organized economy, hunting wild animals, fishing for shellfish or other kinds of fish, with which they sustain themselves collectively. They leave to the care of their women the gathering of seeds, wild and fragrant grasses, and small fruit, which also serve them for sustenance. They sow only tobacco, which is without benefit of curing—but it is not bad tasting.[22]

Their dwellings are small houses of boards with small oval doors, built so as to keep out the winds of the fourth [NW] quadrant which are the coldest and most prevalent.

They also make use of other subterranean dwellings, in the center of which they maintain a fire burning where they offer their sacrifices—although I cannot swear to it.[23] But I can say that they burn their dead and that the eldest among them live here.

The most diligent efforts have not been enough to enable me to acquaint myself with the sect or paganism they follow, and all I know is that the practice of polygamy is unrestrained.

All of the coast, mountains and fields that I surveyed during my stay in this port of Trinidad are covered with a luxuriant growth. Thick, tall, straight pines of the most advantageous quality for ships' curved decking, masts and spars, intermixed with middling white poplar, extend right down to the beach itself, leaving little space for cultivation.

There is so much luxuriant pasturage in these forests, as well as in the small meadows, that I believe numberless cattle could be maintained without difficulty. The plants I was able to identify are wild marjoram, celery, strawberries, mint, honeyberry, verbena, white lilies and roses of Castile. Among the trees are mulberry and blackberry bushes that bear fruit, some yellow and others purple, as in Spain. But they are less sweet than those there.

The temperature is colder than in Europe in this latitude, due, I suspect, to the thick, humid fogs frequently present in the atmosphere. I have formed the opinion that this is the same reason for the abundance of springs. They are encountered everywhere, for in pacing off one hundred and eighty *tuesas* on the beach as a basis for the map I drew, I counted six flowing springs, three of them serving to replenish the ships' water supply. I found the water to be crystal clear. The river's flow is not heavy in this season. Its water is mixed with that of the sea a distance of three to four quarters of a league from its mouth, which is as far up as I went. Its width is about five or six *tuesas*. Inland, its depth permits the floating of the largest launch or the heaviest tree trunk that one might want to convey from the neighboring mountains. Only at the river's mouth will it be necessary to wait for high tide to enter or leave.

Various trees of unusual magnitude,[24] found downed on the landscape adjacent to the river, indicate that floods extend out for one-half to three-quarters of a league, inundating the nearby lowlands, which appear to me most fertile.

The port is enclosed, although it does not appear so on the map because the paper does not extend far enough . The coast continues from the edge of the map, which location I called *Cañada* [ravine], up to a cape which I named *Punta Gorda* [fat point],[25] running NNE—SSW, and extending on a line in this direction that will satisfy anyone as to the port's safety.

Ships should remain moored a distance of eight to ten *varas* from the shore in the area sheltered by the mountain of the cross, and secured with an anchor to the SE, a cable secured on shore to the SW, two moorings at the stern, one to the NE and the other to the N, both on shore, with the precaution of keeping the stern in five-and-one-half *brazas* of water at high tide. In this manner the SW cable is kept from suffering any abrasion, for this bottom is clear while that closer in is full of rocks. Had this information been available in advance I could have prevented the loss of a cable, which was ruined despite having it buoyed.

Shellfish are abundant, but I have not seen any other fish, except for some sardines dried without salt, which the Indians gave us in barter. I was not above trading for them because no fresh meat was left, except that for the sick, and those of us in the cabin were living on rations of jerked beef.

I attribute the limited yield of the sea to this not being the right season. The few fish that are able to remain at this time are hard to catch or are eaten by the sea lions, which are numerous, together with some sea otters.

The tides in all phases of the moon follow just as in the [Atlantic]

Ocean. They have two flood tides and two ebb tides in twenty-four and four-fifths hours. The flood tides are strongest at opposition or full moon; low tides following these are of the same order as on the Cantabrian coast.[26] I was not able to verify if this happens during conjunctions [at new moon] because I left before that happened.

The only difference between these tides and those of Europe is that the two that occur in twenty-four and four-fifths hours are not equal—the one rising and falling little more that half of the other—so that during regular tides the greater rose six to seven Parisian feet and the other four to four-and-one-half feet. At opposition [full moon] the higher tide arrived increasing to ten feet, and the other to five to six feet.

Landfalls on these coasts are not dangerous to make—although the calculation of longitude suffers from great error—if one is warned before approaching it that about one hundred or more leagues out one encounters some *aguas malas*, as they are called in Europe, and which here have the quality of caravels, being rhomboid-shaped, with a crest that looks like a lateen sail.[27] From seventy leagues out other signs are observed that are named *porras*, whose shape is that of a white squash, with the only difference being that the neck extends ten or twelve feet on some, and the head is smaller in relation to those of the squash.[28] Drawing much nearer the land, the sea keeps losing its color, becoming muddy in the vicinity of the coast, so that it looks like a mixture of earth and grasses, some connected to floating roots and woven together with other things into what is called *balsas*.[29]

It is not only these signs that give sure indication the coast is near, but also the birds that they call *centenares*, which become evident at forty leagues. Other birds, that have the shape of a parrot, with a black body and red legs and heads, are sighted at a distance of five to six leagues.[30]

The establishment of a port at Trinidad, besides seeming to me to be advantageous to the extension of the gospel (the first objective of our sovereign), is a virtual necessity not only to secure the convenience it offers to ships of medium size, but also because it would be difficult to dislodge any foreigner who might take possession of it. Its location is inviting to such foreigners for the establishment of a colony, who could then easily deposit their trade goods in the interior of New Mexico, a circumstance that would devolve into well-known detriment to the royal treasury.

The headland of the cross, which I show on the map, is steep in character around its entire circumference, its elevation dominating all the level countryside. This, together with various springs that were seen flowing conspicuously into the sea from this terrain, makes it impregnable if a cut were made in the neck of land connecting it to the mainland where the terrain slopes at a forty-five-degree angle. This same slope would greatly facilitate the operation which I mention.

If a garrison of no more than sixty men were left at the port, there is sufficient land for sown crops and raising livestock so that without any other assistance they would be able to live comfortably without leaving the limits of the fortification, where the quality of the black soil appears to be favorable for farming.

The nineteenth, I left this port with a wind out of the W, and I anchored on the coast two leagues from this port in ten *brazas*. During the time I was in this anchorage the wind was from the NW to the W, and on some occasions was strong.

The twentieth, I set sail in the afternoon, heading the bow from WSW to W, with winds that continued from the NW to the N, freshening and stirring up the sea somewhat.

The twenty-eighth, in the afternoon the winds varied from the second [SE] to the third [SW] quadrant, and became stable out of the west, with dense and damp fogs, that made a large part of my crew ill. Constant attention had to be given to working the ship, because this diminished visibility required that the distance to the schooner be shortened to one or two cable lengths at the most. Despite these precautions, separation was unavoidable on three occasions, although they were only a matter of hours.

The eighth of July, I found myself on the same coast as in the fourth part of M. Bellin's map.[31] This consideration did not interfere with my making the greatest effort day and night, because I was reflecting on how success can come only through diligence. The wind freshened on the night of the 9th, and with an excessively high sea I found myself forced to lay to at twilight because the schooner was unable to push on.

At dawn on the tenth, I sailed hauling the wind, which circled around to N 1/4 NE in full force, and, although the color of the water suggested the nearness of land, we did not manage to see it. I continued on all night with the same determination, but taking every precaution.

The eleventh, at ten-thirty in the morning land was sighted.[32] At two in the afternoon the wind freshened out of the NW, raising a disproportionately high sea, which obliged me to head out to sea, separating myself somewhat from the coast, and to lay to all night. The sea stayed so heavy that it made me drift 40 minutes of latitude from course. At dawn the schooner was six leagues distant off my windward side, and I was about a league from land.[33]

The 12th, when darkness fell, I found myself a league-and-one-half from the coast, with the horizons somewhat changed, and light winds out of the fourth [NW] quadrant. I sounded in eighteen *brazas* and, anticipating the signal, I tacked outward, carrying a full press of sail, so that none of the violent counter currents I was experiencing could run us aground on the coast. At midnight, finding myself in forty *brazas*, I continued lying to in order to wait for the schooner, which I had left behind.

The morning of the 13th, at daybreak, the schooner was at a distance of about five leagues, heading on a course to join me. It allowed itself to come, following along the coast, and anchored at 5:30 in the afternoon in the shelter of a point.[34] A little later it signaled me [warning of] shoals, and, tacking outward, I put the launch in the water, sending it out ahead. I arrived at a small inlet and anchored at nine at night in eight-and-one-half *brazas*, a distance of four to five miles from the schooner.[35] A little later the pilot Don Francisco Maurelle came to this ship, informing me that the schooner found itself surrounded by shoals, and that it needed

The first map of the Washington coast (opposite), showing *Rada de Bucareli* where the landings of 14 July 1775 occurred. The point at B (*Punta de los Mártires*) is almost certainly Cape Elizabeth, south of which the *Sonora* was anchored when seven of its crewmen were killed attempting to land. The nearby river is the Quinault, and the dots extending south of B show the reef on which the *Sonora* was temporarily stranded. Hezeta's party landed at A (*Situación de la Cruz*), near an island marked C (*Isla del Desembarco*). Another island is shown at D (*Isla del Engaño*). The island at C is apparently one of several rocky islets within Grenville Bay, and the island at D is probably Grenville Arch, lying off Point Grenville.

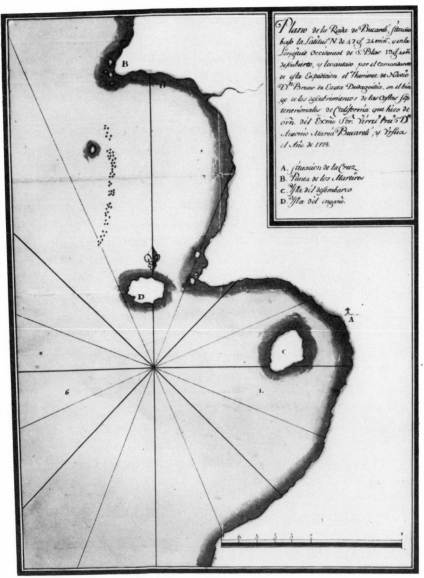

The inscription reads:

Map of Bucareli's roadstead, located below latitude N 47[°]24', and in longitude west of San Blas 19[°]40', discovered and charted by the commander of this expedition, first lieutenant Don Bruno de [H]ezeta Dudagoitia, on the voyage of discoveries to the northern coasts of California, which was made by order of His Excellency, the Viceroy, Frey Don Antonio María Bucareli y Ursúa in the year 1775.

|   |   |
|---|---|
| A. Location of the cross | C. Landing island |
| B. Martyrs' point | D. Deceit island |

(Archivo General de Indias, Sevilla. OHS neg.#67613)

daylight to get itself free. I put him in charge of carrying this out without losing a moment.

The morning of the 14th dawned with misty horizons that did not permit us to make out the schooner. At four-thirty in the morning, I landed accompanied by the Reverend Father Fray Benito de la Sierra, Don Cristóbal Revilla, the surgeon Don Juan Gonzales, and some armed men.[36] I took possession at six in the morning (following the Instructions strictly in every detail), giving it the name Rada de Bucareli [Bucareli's roadstead], and returned at seven-thirty in the morning.[37]

Only six Indians presented themselves to me ashore, young fellows, unarmed, who traded salmon, red gurnard and other kinds of fish for glass beads. One of them was dressed in a red chamois skin.[38]

These Indians, like another nine that I left at the frigate when I departed on this mission, have beautiful faces. Some are fair in color, others dark and all of them plump and well built. Their clothing consists of sea otter skins with which they cover themselves from the waist up. I figure that this was more a matter of prevention—to defend themselves—than the need to keep themselves warm.

The beach was surrounded by an extremely dense grove of pine trees, which were not particularly tall or big around. It is not hard to believe that this is the result of their growing so close together. Besides this, the clearings were choked with brush and branches so that any object at a distance of four varas can not be seen by anyone outside.

The seas on these coasts rise higher than anywhere except the gulfs. This is due to the fact that they are all soundable, so that at a distance of six leagues one finds from sixty to seventy varas, diminishing ten varas for each league that one approaches land.

Another thing that helps a great deal to cause high seas is the fact that the currents are more violent in these places. So, when the tide comes in, the actions of the sea break and foam over and over, because then the currents move in the opposite direction from the seas, which are raised by the winds of the fourth [NW] quadrant, the ones that generally prevail on the coast. When the tide goes out the current is much faster toward the second [SE] quadrant than the first [NE] quadrant, when it comes in. I have ob-

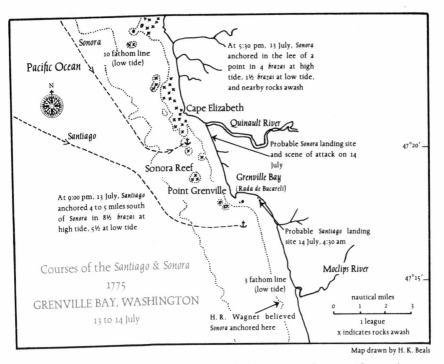

At 5:30 pm, 13 July, *Sonora* anchored in the lee of a point in 4 *brazas* at high tide, 1½ *brazas* at low tide, and nearby rocks awash

Pacific Ocean

*Sonora*

10 fathom line (low tide)

*Santiago*

Cape Elizabeth

Quinault River

Probable *Sonora* landing site and scene of attack on 14 July

47°20′

Sonora Reef

Point Grenville

Grenville Bay (*Rada de Bucareli*)

At 9:00 pm, 13 July, *Santiago* anchored 4 to 5 miles south of *Sonora* in 8½ *brazas* at high tide, 5½ at low tide

Probable *Santiago* landing site 14 July, 4:30 am

Courses of the *Santiago* & *Sonora*

1775

GRENVILLE BAY, WASHINGTON

13 to 14 July

Moclips River

47°15′

3 fathom line (low tide)

H. R. Wagner believed *Sonora* anchored here

nautical miles

0   1   2   3

1 league

x indicates rocks awash

Map drawn by H. K. Beals

served that both tides are more rapid three to six leagues from the coast than out beyond eight leagues.

I observed the tide was just like that which I mentioned at Trinidad, with the only difference being that here the greatest waxing and waning is thirteen feet.

The sea swell rose in proportion to the advancing day. The wind was calm, keeping me from being able to set sail, and all I could do was get ready to take advantage of the wind by putting in the launch and recovering the cable.

At eleven in the morning I sighted the schooner which was still anchored but diligently making an effort to set sail. At twelve-thirty their swivel guns were fired, and I, figuring that it was in danger from the nearby shoals, sent the launch with a stream anchor and cable. At two, seeing that it was joining us, I unfurled the topsails, placing myself in a risky situation, and alone I awaited impatiently to find out what event had made them call for help in order to set sail. Its commander informed me by word of mouth and in writing of the following:

*In the morning of that day, at low tide, exactly at seven in the morning, what happened was that* [the schooner] *found itself surrounded entirely by shoals, and*

77

*consequently could not join us until high tide. In this interval, it was decided to replenish the water supply and to cut some poles for the main topsail masts. To do this, it had sent the boatswain with six other well-armed men.*[39] *When they arrived on land, some three hundred Indians, falling upon them treacherously, had surrounded the boat and knifed those who were in it (so far as we know), with the exception of two men who threw themselves in the water, defending themselves. But they turned back towards land exhausted, and they* [the crewmen aboard the schooner] *did not know whether it was reached or whether afterward they suffered the same martyrdom as their mates.*[40]

That the Indians had shown great gentleness in their manner, like that of the Indians at Trinidad, had brought their women on board this morning, and having exchanged meat and fish of different kinds for the presents of glass beads that had been given them, all [seemingly were] signs of true and sincere friendship between them [Bodega's crew and the Indians].

Despite this account of what happened, I set sail in order to get more depth. Meanwhile, in the confusion, we were trying to decide whether or not those treacherous people should be punished; and also whether the schooner should continue on, considering that on the eleventh, as mentioned above, it was not able to endure the seas without lying to with extreme difficulty.

As to the first proposal, the commander and pilot were of the opinion that the Indians should be punished. Don Juan Pérez and Don Cristóbal Revilla were opposed. I went along with the latter two. This was because, in the first place, I am guided by Article 23 of the Instructions: not to give offense except in case of the need for self-defense.

Secondly, from what I knew of the terrain I realized we were in no position to inflict injury but rather to receive it.

In the third place, I was opposed because I had a lot of sick men, and the least loss of manpower would have forced us to give up the mission.

In the fourth place, in attempting it, the only way to assure some advantage would have been in catching them unawares, for any other way they would have had the advantage of being able to advance or retreat because they were experienced in covering that wild terrain, and they would have been in a position to ambush us continually.

In the fifth place, in order to gain that distance to windward, it would have been necessary to spend several days, which, besides giving them a chance to muster their forces in better order, would also have delayed the mission; and because on our return it could offer us an advantageous occasion, as happened to me, which will be described in its place.

In reference to the second point, as to whether or not the schooner should continue farther northward, its commander and pilot, together with Don Juan Pérez, were of the opinion that it was well able to proceed on. Being in agreement with this opinion, I replaced the crew that had been lost with one from the frigate, and we set our course turning to the W in order to gain longitude.

From the fourteenth to the nineteenth of July we experienced calm winds out of the fourth [NW] quadrant, with colorful skies and heavy clouds that promised no trouble, except that on the sixteenth we got light winds out of the third [SW] quadrant.

On this day, the nineteenth, the second officer, Don Juan Pérez, submitted the following petition to me:

*My Dear Sir: With attention to the laws of the sea and my obligations as first pilot, and pilot of this voyage, I must inform Your Excellency that despite the great effort that we have made we have not been able to bring ourselves to a higher latitude in quite a long time because of having had diametrically opposite winds, stronger than those we experienced last year, which are continuing at the present. The season is far advanced, and if later on contrary winds burden us, we will not have time to return, because in order to ascend to the latitude of 50°, depending on the weather we experience, we need at least a month. Besides this, we are short-handed and the men are very exhausted; many are sick. We scarcely have enough men available to work the ship, and if some weather should burden us we would be endangered from a shortage of men.*

*Praise be to God our Lord*
*On board the frigate*
*19 July 1775*
*Don Juan Pérez*

I had the surgeon, Don Juan Gonzales, certify the number of sick, which amounted to twenty-nine. Having requested opinions from from the commander and pilot of the schooner (who favored continuing on for a time) plus from Don Cristóbal de Revilla (who was for running before the wind) I yielded to the first two, availing myself of the winds of the fourth [NW] quadrant and moderating the sail in accordance with the escort.

The 24th, all the ship's officers [aboard the *Santiago*] represented to me in writing the same things as Don Juan Pérez, but I, with a desire to push on, continued even though I would not be able to attain all that I had been ordered to do by the Instructions.

At six in the evening, the wind having veered to the WNW, I tacked in order to gain latitude, and I maintained this tack with winds out of the W to WNW until the 28th. On this day, having gone far enough to gain the latitude expressed in the Table [48°44'], the wind swung to the N, and I tacked as required from the WNW.

The 28th of July, toward nightfall, seeing that the wind freshened and that the heavy sea kept the schooner from staying on course, which the frigate's rigging permitted me to do, I continued to lay to in order to prevent the separation which would have been inevitable had I not done so.

Dawn broke on the 29th with squally skies, the sea and wind strong, and the schooner some five leagues windward. It arrived and joined us at noon. I lay to all this day because the sea and wind had gotten stronger. I lost sight of the schooner at ten in the evening.

Dawn broke on the 30th with misty horizons. I waited until ten in the morning. Once the day cleared up and finding no trace of the schooner, I called a meeting of Don Juan Pérez, Don Cristóbal de Revilla, and all the ship's officers in order that they might give me their opinion in writing as to what ought to be done. All were for running before the wind because of the few men left to work the ship. Not being able to go along with this opinion, I determined to veer toward land, for I figured on meeting the schooner in that area. I continued on, turning to E 1/4 NE, with the wind out of the N, and the same heavy sea that impeded attaining a more advantageous course.

The second of August, with variable winds out of the fourth [NW] quadrant, I began to gain latitude.

The fifth, the winds began to wheel around to the third [SW] quadrant, with continuous heavy showers, and I took advantage of

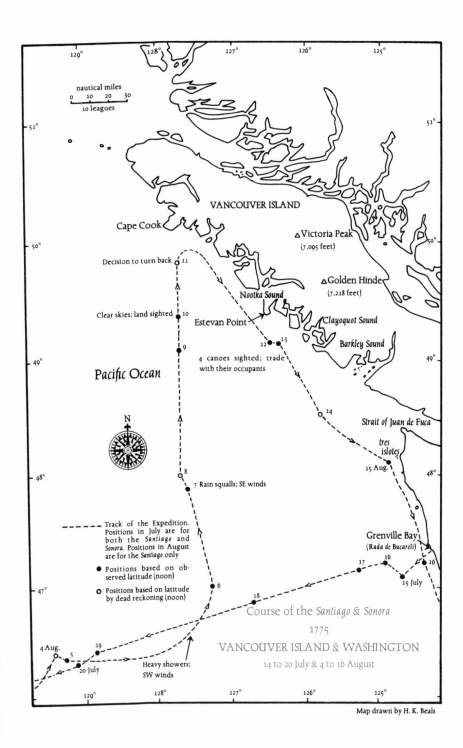

nautical miles
0   10   20   30
10 leagues

129°    128°    127°    126°    125°

51°

VANCOUVER ISLAND

Cape Cook

△Victoria Peak
(7,095 feet)

50°

Decision to turn back ○ 11

△Golden Hinde
(7,218 feet)

Clear skies; land sighted ● 10

Nootka Sound

Estevan Point

Clayoquot Sound

● 9

Barkley Sound

12 ●● 13

4 canoes sighted; trade
with their occupants

49°

Pacific Ocean

N

14
○

Strait of Juan de Fuca

tres
islotes

15 Aug. ○

48°

○ 8

● 7 Rain squalls; SE winds

Grenville Bay
(Rada de Bucareli)

Track of the Expedition.
Positions in July are for
both the *Santiago* and
*Sonora*. Positions in August
are for the *Santiago* only

17    16 ○

○ 16

●  Positions based on ob-
served latitude (noon)

15 July

○  Positions based on latitude
by dead reckoning (noon)

47°

○ 6

18 ○

Course of the *Santiago* & *Sonora*

4 Aug. ○

19 ○

1775

5 ●

VANCOUVER ISLAND & WASHINGTON

20 July

Heavy showers;
SW winds

14 to 20 July & 4 to 16 August

129°    128°    127°    126°    125°

Map drawn by H. K. Beals

them to go up. The seventh they veered to the second [SE quadrant], with continuing rain squalls and darkened horizons.

The 10th, the winds died down completely, the horizons cleared up and I sighted land.[41] I took bearings on the direction of the coast from latitude 50°40′ down to 49°50′; it extended through an angle of 38° of the second [SE] quadrant.

There are some high mountains in the interior of this coast, which have quite a lot of snow in their ravines. They make prominent landmarks, easily recognizable because amongst them two stand out particularly well viewed from the SE toward the NW. One looks like the peak of Tenerife, and it is situated in latitude 50°. The other is like the *Cuchillada de Roldán* [slash of Roland] (on the coast of Valencia), and this one is in latitude 49°30′.[42]

The mountains close to shore are low, and they are only seen clearly close in.

The eleventh, the second pilot Don Cristóbal Revilla, with all the ship's officers, presented me a statement that in substance says:

*The sailors were getting so sick that only a few were able to serve on watch; and of these most are scurvy-ridden and unable to attend working the ship; and thus, on one of the extremely critical days that often occur at sea, the ship and its crew were, as all well knew, exposed to the risk of perishing.*

In the presence of Don Cristóbal, I discussed this statement with second captain, Don Juan Pérez. He responded that he had said the same thing to me in writing on the 19th of last month; that in his judgment to go up to latitude 51° or 52° would inevitably mean serious loss, because he knew that if the rain squalls continued, which he experienced last year in those heights, it would completely exhaust the crew that was left to us, and that the crew was no longer sufficient to make it back.

In view of these statements, the condition of the crew and the winds having veered this morning to the fourth [NW] quadrant, which were adverse to gaining latitude, I determined to approach the coast in order to follow it, examining closely its bearings, ports, inlets and so forth, before the few crewmen I had left became completely useless, requiring me to make another less extended voyage.

The 12th, although dawn came with gloomy horizons, it cleared up at intervals, allowing the coast to be seen down to its shorelines, and I took bearings from latitude 49°45' down to 49°. The two most prominent capes extend through an angle of 36 degrees of the second [SE] quadrant.

An inlet is formed between these two most prominent capes that extends inland for three or four leagues.[43] The coast terminates in a beach, and the mountains immediately adjoining these capes are low.

Between eight and nine in the morning four canoes of Indians were sighted that were making every effort to approach this ship. At ten they came alongside. After being off the stern for about a quarter of an hour, observing the movements we made, giving many outcries, the oldest of them speaking with discordant voices unintelligible to us, they bartered some sea otter pelts with the sailors and, with me, one of the canoes in which they came. Although their forms are very advantageous to cut the water, they are extremely frail and light, and only by keeping them well-balanced—in which those Indians are highly skilled—are they fit for navigation.[44]

I noted that they are extremely deceptive in trading. After they had reached agreement on the canoe and the pledge was handed over to them, they wanted to leave with it.[45] But, by threatening them with a musket, they delivered it over, a circumstance that has persuaded me they have some knowledge of that weapon—no doubt, ever since the incident with the schooner, mentioned on 14 July in 47°26'. Their look and clothing are completely like those at that latitude. They possess the same inclination for iron as at Trinidad.

The 14th and 15th of August, I came sailing along the coast from 49°30' to 48°, sounding at various times, the bottom of which, besides being clear of sand and mud, affirms to the navigator how close he is to land.

I ran all along this coast through an angle of 30° of the second [SE] quadrant. In the latitude of 48°4', a distance of one league from the land, there are three small islands of moderate height.[46] And in 47°58' is situated the island that I named *Dolores* [sorrows], which is half a league distant from the mainland. It has a circumference of

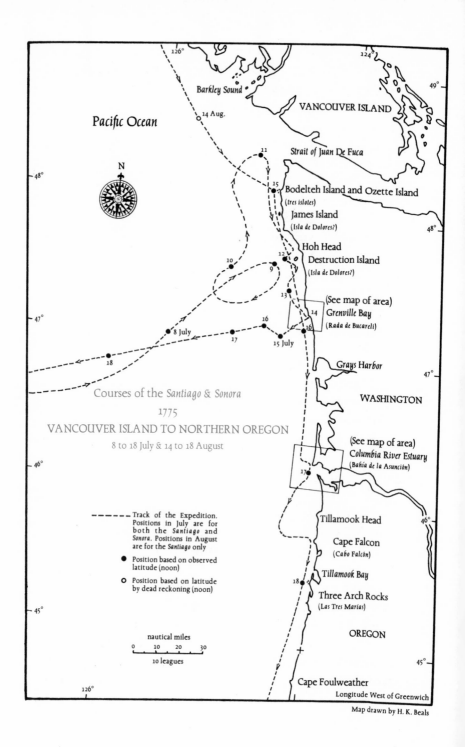

126°

Barkley Sound

Pacific Ocean

14 Aug.

VANCOUVER ISLAND

124°

49°

Strait of Juan De Fuca

11

N

48°

15

Bodeltch Island and Ozette Island
(tres islotes)

James Island
(Isla de Dolores?)

48°

Hoh Head

12

10

9

Destruction Island
(Isla de Dolores?)

13

(See map of area)
Grenville Bay
(Rada de Bucareli)

14

47°

16

16

8 July

17

15 July

Grays Harbor

47°

18

WASHINGTON

Courses of the *Santiago* & *Sonora*

1775

VANCOUVER ISLAND TO NORTHERN OREGON

8 to 18 July & 14 to 18 August

(See map of area)
Columbia River Estuary
(Bahía de la Asunción)

46°

17

46°

Tillamook Head

- - - - - Track of the Expedition.
Positions in July are for
both the *Santiago* and
*Sonora*. Positions in August
are for the *Santiago* only

Cape Falcon
(Cabo Falcón)

● Position based on observed
latitude (noon)

Tillamook Bay

18

○ Position based on latitude
by dead reckoning (noon)

Three Arch Rocks
(Las Tres Marías)

45°

OREGON

nautical miles

0    10    20    30

10 leagues

45°

126°

Cape Foulweather

Longitude West of Greenwich

Map drawn by H. K. Beals

about a league and one half, being populated by a dense grove of pine trees; it is rectangularly shaped, level and little elevated.[47]

The afternoon of this day, the 15th, finding myself in latitude 47°34', a canoe with ten Indians came alongside at four in the afternoon, ready to barter dried sardines and pelts with some of the crew of this frigate. The crewmen said that they recognized two of them who were the same ones that had come to this ship on the 14th of July in the *Rada de Bucareli*, and who had been accomplices in the treachery that happened at the schooner on that day as mentioned above.

I intended to get hold of them, without violence, with the purpose of taking them to the scene of that unhappy event to offer them in an exchange for the return of any of the men who had sustained the assault, if by chance any were still alive.

I invited them to come aboard, but they refused to do it. I let them become engaged in trade until there was an opportunity to seize them with the grappling iron of the launch, which weighs six *arrobas*. But they, being exceedingly dexterous and strong, hurled it into the water. [This happened] despite the force that a weight of this nature attains in falling from a height of six-and-one-half *varas* and the damage it might have done a canoe of such light weight, having struck it with the claws. Nor did it injure one of the Indians who suffered part of the blow—and he was the same one who flung it off.

I tried to frighten them with musket shots which I ordered fired in the air, so that they would head for land in confusion where it would have been easy for me to overtake them. But they always steered into the wind where it was impossible for me to reach. I lost them from sight at sundown.

The 16th, I observed that the coast continued through an angle of 18° of the second [SE] quadrant. From 48° down to 47°, it all terminates in a forested shore, with a depth of sixty *brazas* at a distance of six or seven leagues, which diminishes a *braza* per each league as one approaches land.

There are some rocky headlands and small islands distributed in the immediate vicinity of the coast that are numerous, but little exposed for the mariner, so I did not take the extra trouble to locate their corresponding latitudes.

The 17th, I passed along the coast down to 46° and saw that, from the latitude of 47°4' down to 46°40', it ran through an angle of 18° of the second [SE] quadrant and from that latitude down to 46°4' through an angle of 12° of the same quadrant, with the same depth, shore, luxuriant vegetation and some small islands as on the previous days.

In the afternoon of this day I discovered a large bay that I named *Bahía de la Asunción* [assumption bay], the shape of which is shown on the map that is going to be inserted in this diary. Its latitude and extent are subject to the most exact determinations that theory and practice offer in this career.[48]

The latitudes of the most prominent capes of said bay, particularly the one on the N., are calculated from the observation of this day.

Having arrived alongside the bay at six in the evening, with the frigate placed almost midway between the two capes, I sounded in 24 *brazas*. The swirling currents were so swift that despite having a full press of sail it was difficult to get clear or separate myself from the cape to the extreme N., toward which the current tended to run, its direction also being to the E., depending on the tidal flow.

These currents and the seething of the waters have led me to believe that it may be the mouth of some great river or some passage to another sea.[49]

---

The first map of the Columbia River estuary (opposite), showing *Bahía de la Asunción* discovered and so named by Hezeta on 17 August 1775. It was also later referred to as *Entrada de Hezeta*. An island depicted at B, bearing the name *Cabo de San Roque*, is modern Cape Disappointment. It is in fact not an island, although it appears so from off shore. Another point at C (*Cabo Frondoso*) has been variously identified as Point Adams and Tillamook Head. The inscription reads:

Map of Assumption bay or [H]ezeta's entrance, located below latitude N 46[°]00', discovered and charted by the commander of this expedition, first lieutenant Don Bruno de [H]ezeta Dudagoitia, on the voyage of discoveries to the northern coasts of California, which was made by order of His Excellency, the Viceroy, Frey Don Antonio María Bucareli y Ursúa in the year 1775.

A. Assumption bay                                    B. San Roque's cape
C. Cape luxuriant
(Archivo General de Indias, Sevilla. OHS neg.#48234)

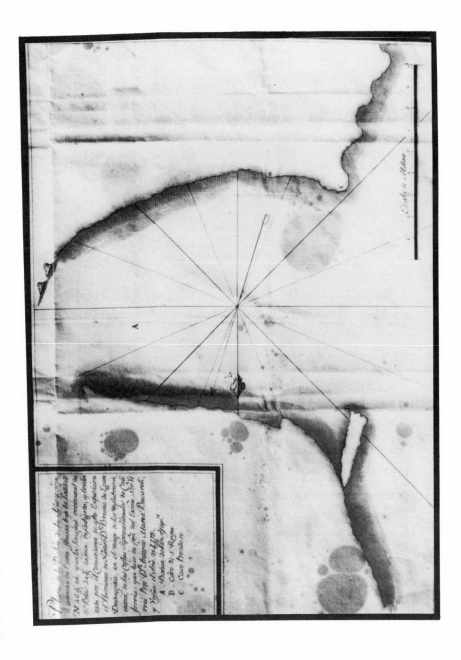

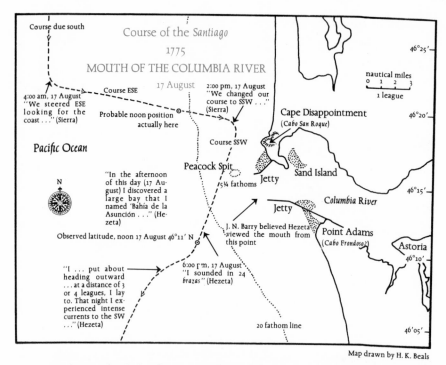

Course due south

Course of the *Santiago*

1775

MOUTH OF THE COLUMBIA RIVER

17 August

Course ESE

4:00 am, 17 August "We steered ESE looking for the coast..." (Sierra)

2:00 pm, 17 August "We changed our course to SSW..." (Sierra)

Probable noon position actually here

Cape Disappointment *(Cabo San Roque)*

46°25'

nautical miles
0   1   2   3

1 league

46°20'

Pacific Ocean

"In the afternoon of this day (17 August) I discovered a large bay that I named 'Bahía de la Asunción...'" (Hezeta)

Course SSW

Peacock Spit

5¼ fathoms

Jetty

Sand Island

Columbia River

46°15'

N

Jetty

Observed latitude, noon 17 August 46°11' N

J. N. Barry believed Hezeta viewed the mouth from this point

Point Adams *(Cabo Frondoso?)*

Astoria

46°10'

"I ... put about heading outward ... at a distance of 3 or 4 leagues, I lay to. That night I experienced intense currents to the SW ..." (Hezeta)

6:00 pm, 17 August "I sounded in 24 *brazas*" (Hezeta)

20 fathom line

46'05'

Map drawn by H. K. Beals

Had I not had the firm evidence of the observation of that day as to the latitude in which the bay is located, I might have readily believed it to be the passage discovered in the year 1692 by Juan de Fuca,[50] which is located on the maps between 48° and 47° latitude; where I am certain no such strait exists, for I anchored on the 14th of July in the middle of these latitudes and I examined on various occasions everything thereabouts.

Despite the considerable difference in the position of this bay and the passage mentioned by de Fuca, it is rather difficult to doubt that it is the same one, because there is equal or greater variation observed in the latitudes of other capes and parts of this coast, as will be mentioned in its proper time. In all instances, the latitude given for them is greater than their true positions.

I did not enter and anchor in the port that appears on the map, formed by what I suppose is an island, despite my ardent desire to do so.[51] This was because, having taken the opinion of second captain and pilot Don Juan Pérez and that of pilot Don Cristóbal Revilla, they insisted that I should not attempt it, for in letting go the anchor we did not have men with which to get it up, nor to attend to the work that would thereby result. Considering these reasons, and that in order to head into the anchorage I would have to put in the launch (the only boat I had) and man it with at least fourteen members of the crew, without whom I could not commit myself, and noting at the same time that it was late, I resolved to put about heading outward. Finding myself at a distance of three or four leagues, I lay to. That night I experienced intense currents to the SW that made it impossible for me to attempt to enter this bay on the following morning, being far to leeward. These currents likewise convinced me that at ebb tide a great quantity of water issues from this bay.

The two capes shown on the map as *San Roque* and *Frondoso* [luxuriant] run through an angle of 10° of the third [SW] quadrant; both are steep, of ruddy earth and little elevated.[52]

The 18th, I surveyed the *Cabo Frondoso*, which is situated with another cape that I named *Falcón* located in latitude 45°43′, running through an angle of 22 degrees of the third [SW] quadrant.[53] Beyond this cape the coast continues through an angle of 5° of the second [SE] quadrant. This land is mountainous but not very elevated, nor as well forested as that from latitude 48°30′ down to 46°.

In sounding I found considerable difference, for at a distance of seven leagues I sounded in 84 *varas* but as I approached the coast I sometimes found no bottom. This leads me to believe there are some reefs or sandbanks on this coast, which is also shown by the color of the water.[54] In some places the coast ends in a beach, and in others in steep cliffs.

A level mountain, which I named *La Mesa* [the table], will enable any navigator to be sure of the position of *Cabo Falcón*, even if it could not be observed, for it is in latitude 45°28′, and it can be seen at a considerable distance, being fairly high.[55]

In the latitude of 45°30′ there are three rocky headlands or hillocks that I named *Las Tres Marías* [the three Marys].[56]

The 19th, I took bearings on the coast down to 43°20′ for navigation and some survey determinations, running through an angle of 5° of the second [SE] quadrant. The coast is moderately elevated, the mountains being rather broken and covered with fairly luxuriant vegetation.

The 20th, morning dawned with clear horizons, slightly misty, and the wind fresh out of the N. Considering that in the latitude of 43° is where the maps place Aguilar's river, I made every effort to

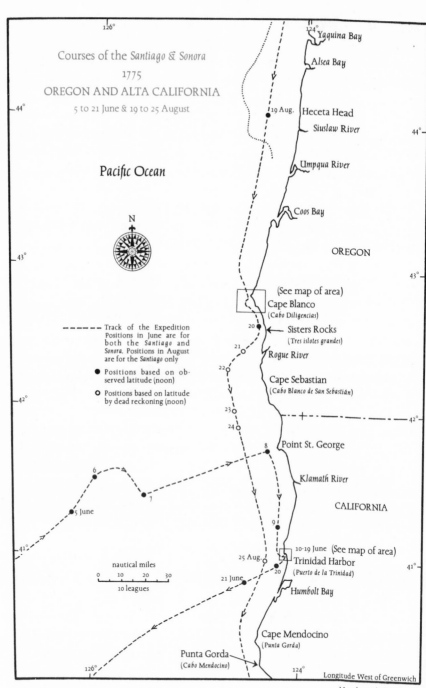

Courses of the *Santiago* & *Sonora*
1775
OREGON AND ALTA CALIFORNIA
5 to 21 June & 19 to 25 August

Pacific Ocean

N

Yaquina Bay

Alsea Bay

19 Aug. Heceta Head
Siuslaw River

Umpqua River

Coos Bay

OREGON

(See map of area)
Cape Blanco
(*Cabo Diligencias*)

20 ← Sisters Rocks
(*Tres islotes grandes*)

21

Rogue River

22

Cape Sebastian
(*Cabo Blanco de San Sebastián*)

- - - - - Track of the Expedition
Positions in June are for
both the *Santiago* and
*Sonora*. Positions in August
are for the *Santiago* only

● Positions based on ob-
served latitude (noon)

○ Positions based on latitude
by dead reckoning (noon)

23

24

8 Point St. George

Klamath River

6

7

CALIFORNIA

5 June

9

10-19 June (See map of area)
25 Aug. Trinidad Harbor
20 (*Puerto de la Trinidad*)

21 June

Humbolt Bay

nautical miles

0   10   20   30
10 leagues

Cape Mendocino
(*Punta Gorda*)

Punta Gorda
(*Cabo Mendocino*)

Longitude West of Greenwich

Map drawn by H. K. Beals

90

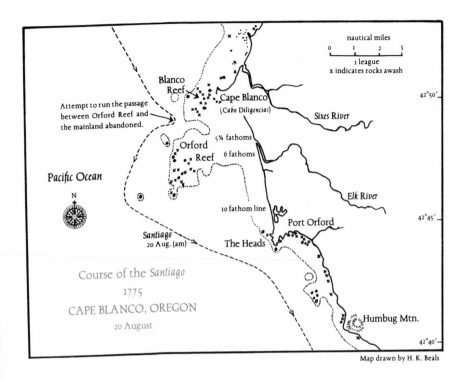

Blanco
Reef

Cape Blanco
(*Cabo Diligencias*)

Sixes River

Attempt to run the passage
between Orford Reef and
the mainland abandoned.

42°50'

5¼ fathoms

Orford
Reef    6 fathoms

Pacific Ocean

N

Elk River

10 fathom line

Port Orford

42°45'

Santiago
20 Aug. (am)

The Heads

Course of the *Santiago*

1775

CAPE BLANCO, OREGON

20 August

Humbug Mtn.

42°40'

Map drawn by H. K. Beals

approach as near as possible to the coast with the purpose of discovering it.[57]

I examined the vicinity of this latitude closely, but all I found
were some small islands, numbering ten, about a league-and-one-
half distant from the land. I set a course in order to pass through
the channel between them and the mainland, but I was warned by
the lookout at the masthead of other rocks being seen level with
the sea, and of coming very close to running aground on them.[58]
Sailing past them, I approached the coast again and continued examining it until one-thirty in the afternoon, without which it
might have been able to conceal its less commendable features.[59]

Finding myself now in latitude 42°30', based on the observation
of this noon, the location of the Cabo Blanco de San Sebastián, according to the distance it appeared to me, was to be found in latitude 42°10' and runs in the direction of the coast through an angle
of 6° of the second [SE] quadrant.[60]

Note

The maps of M. Bellin and Father Miguel Venegas place this cape
in latitudes 43° and in 43°20'.[61]

91

A cape is found in latitude 42°58', which I named Diligencias [diligence],[62] and which is by the small islands mentioned above that extended out more than a league; the center of these small islands by the cape runs through an angle of 45° of the third [SW] quadrant, a distance of two leagues.

From latitude 43°20' down to 42°50' the coast is low; from there it begins to be moderately mountainous, and in the latitude of this day's observation, which must be 42°36', there are three large islets very close to the mainland.[63]

At two in the afternoon the wind fell calm, and suddenly a heavy sea came up out of the W, which was troublesome to me because I was in an inlet. A little later, all the horizons having clouded over, a little wind came up out of the SE, so that, availing myself of it with all my power, I put myself in a good sailing position.

The sea out of the W began to subside at three-thirty, with which I avoided the risk I might have faced had the wind and sea combined.

I continued at the will of the currents, which follow the immediate vicinity of the coast, descending to the S, with heavy fog on the horizons and light winds out of the second [SE] and third [SW] quadrants, until the 25th. At that time, the weather having cleared with a NW wind, I set a course to approach the land. Having calculated the observation for this day, I found that the currents carried me seventy miles to the S.

The 26th, I made landfall off Cabo Mendocino, located by the observation of that day in latitude 40°7'. This cape falls precipitously into the sea, and it displays four cliffs of ruddy earth with some small trees on the slopes.[64]

Note

The map of M. Bellin and the Historia de Californias locate this cape in 42°.[65]

From Cabo Blanco de San Sebastián down to Cabo Mendocino, although with no chance of examining any place in between, I made for the port of Trinidad, running from Cabo Blanco de San Sebastián through an angle of 22° of the second [SE] quadrant; from there to Punta Gorda, through 20° of the third [SW] quadrant; and from this point to Cabo Mendocino, through 10° of the second [SE] quadrant—all of it covered with forest.

The Mission of San Carlos Borromeo as depicted in an engraving from a sketch made in 1794, appearing in George Vancouver's journals. In September and October, 1775, Hezeta's ailing crewmen recovered from their ordeal at sea either here or at the nearby presidio on Monterey Bay.

(From George Vancouver, A *Voyage of Discovery to the North Pacific Ocean and Round the World . . . Performed in Years 1790 . . . 1795*, Vol. II., 1801. OHS neg. #67568)

At two this afternoon, it became foggy, and despite sailing a very short distance off the coast the shore was but poorly discerned. At nightfall, I headed the bow away from the coast and made sail to reach the vicinity of the port of San Francisco in order to enter it in fulfillment of the orders with which I was charged. I judged that, although the shortage of hands as a result of the many who were sick might prevent me from being able to depart, I could always easily get help from the sailors at Monterey.

At noon on the 27th, the latitude was observed to be 37°51′, with the horizons clear, and strong winds out of the NW. I set a course to the NNE and made landfall at eight in the evening very close to land in latitude 38°16′, according to my dead reckoning.[66] With the same clear horizons, I stayed off a little all that night tacking so as not to separate myself from the land.

The 28th, at two in the morning the horizons were shrouded in exceedingly dense fog; at four, going on a tack landward, I sounded in 20 *brazas*, and tacked outward to allow time for the fog to dissi-

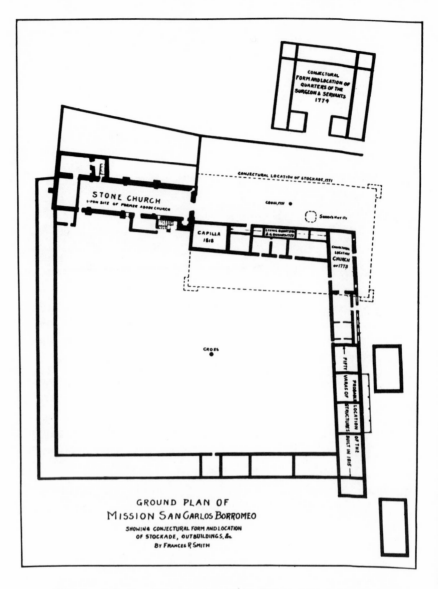

GROUND PLAN OF
MISSION SAN CARLOS BORROMEO
SHOWING CONJECTURAL FORM AND LOCATION
OF STOCKADE, OUTBUILDINGS, &
BY FRANCES R SMITH

The ground plan of Mission San Carlos Borromeo as reconstructed by Frances R. Smith in 1921. If Hezeta's men were accommodated here, as seems likely, it would have been in the area enclosed in the dotted line and labeled "conjectural location of stockade 1771," or possibly the structure identified as "conjectural form and location of quarters of the surgeon & servants 1774."

(From Frances Rand Smith, *The Architectural History of Mission San Carlos Borromeo*, 1921. OHS neg.#71833)

94

pate. At six in the morning, I re-tacked again landward, and at eight I saw breakers that I judged to be from the bar of some river. Because I could not make out the beach, which was far from the breakers and about a quarter-of-a-league from this frigate, I came about in order to stay outside.[67] I now called Don Juan Pérez and Don Cristóbal Revilla to the cabin, and requested their opinion as to whether we ought to persist in seeking the port of San Francisco. They responded that there was no excuse to, because otherwise we would find ourselves in danger from the bar. At ten I sighted the Farallones,[68] and I assembled them [Pérez and Revilla] again asking them the same thing. They responded as mentioned before, because the land was shrouded in fog. At that time, I surveyed the Farallones, and they bore to the SSW. I set the bow on a course SW 1/4S, hauling the wind the whole time, despite taking a course so advantageous for passing windward of them. The current went toward the S so strongly that I had to be extremely careful to get above them. The sky cleared at 11:00, and at noon I observed the latitude at 37°49'.

Although the sky was clear, the horizons continued to be foggy, particularly those landward.

At two in the afternoon I found myself far beyond the SE Farallones. The sky turned cloudy, with conditions that limited visibility to a musket shot. Despairing of reaching the above-mentioned port of San Francisco, I set a course for Monterey, where I anchored at four in the afternoon on the 29th.

The following day I made arrangements with the infirmary, and on the 31st I transferred thirty-five sick men. One of them, named Antonio Esteban, died being carried there. Besides these, the men remaining on board were scurvy-ridden. Other ailing ones, numbering as many as ten, were all much improved with the refreshments they were furnished at the Presidio of Monterey, Mission of San Carlos.

The 14th of September, I departed the port of Monterey accompanied by an escort of 10 soldiers, who were assigned to go over to San Francisco. I took four sailors and a canoe with which I had to explore and prepare a map of the port. Meanwhile, the crewmen who were left sick experienced improvement. I arrived on the 21st and having found various letters of Don Juan de Ayala which stated fully all of the reconnaissance he had done, I returned to the port of Monterey on the 1st of October.[69]

At the point that forms the S. part of this port [of San Francisco], I observed the latitude of its entrance to be 37°54', although I am not completely certain of it. The Farallones are at an angle of 82°30' of the third [SW] quadrant. The Punta de los Reyes is 59° of the 4th [NW quadrant], and the Punta de las Almejas is 6° of the third [SW] quadrant.[70]

### Note

This port is located in latitude 38°45' by the map of M. Bellin.

The 7th, the schooner anchored in this port [of Monterey] with the captain Don Juan Francisco la Quadra, pilot Don Francisco Maurelle and all its gear and sick crewmen. I had to stay over in this port until they had recovered and were somewhat rested from so arduous a cruise. On the 1st of November, at nine in the morning, I weighed anchor bound for the port of San Blas. Finding myself outside the points,[71] the winds with which I had departed fell calm, so that I was within sight of the port until the 4th, when we got a wind out of the NW. With it, I followed the necessary headings to keep clear of the islands,[72] and I made landfall on the coast in the evening of the 13th at about latitude 24°30'. On the 16th, at six in the evening, I left Cabo San Lucas behind,[73] which I consider below latitude 22°48'.

The 18th, at six in the evening, I saw the Islas Marías, and on the 20th I cast anchor in the port of San Blas, warping that same evening into the anchorage.

On board the frigate *Galicia* in the port of San Blas
20 November 1775
Bruno de Hezeta

# FOR HONOR AND COUNTRY
## EPILOGUE

# EPILOGUE

Fray Benito de la Sierra wrote at the conclusion of his account of the Hezeta expedition, "Thanks be to God who brought us safely through so many perils."[1] But for Antonio Esteban, the sailor who died while being carried ashore at Monterey, there would be no thankful homecoming. Hezeta's laconic entry in his *Diario* records only the unfortunate sailor's name and the fact of his death; Sierra adds that he was buried in the chapel at the presidio in Monterey.

As for the survivors, they seem to have recovered quickly enough. Many of them evidently recuperated at the Mission of San Carlos Borromeo, on the Carmel River, some distance to the south of the presidio, for Sierra remarks that once Esteban's interment had been accomplished "We then went to the Mission of Carmel."[2] Under the gentle ministerings of its Franciscan fathers, Junípero Serra, Juan Crespi and Francisco Palóu, the crew's spirits and health no doubt quickly revived.

Years later, in 1793, after both Serra and Crespi had themselves been interred in the soil of this missionary outpost, construction of a stone church was begun there. Its two bell towers, one with a large, rounded, Moorish dome, the other square and smaller, remain to this day silent reminders of the Spanish presence that once enlivened these shores. No one knows how many of Hezeta's officers or men ever returned to see this ecclesiastical landmark or enter its sacred precincts. But they could take justifiable pride in the role they had played in assuring that such an edifice was built there.

The burial of Antonio Esteban was by no means the only such unhappy event at which Father Sierra and his colleague, Fray Miguel de la Campa Cos, had presided. They were well acquainted with burials at sea on the arduous voyage that had just been completed. Yet there was perhaps no sadder entry in Sierra's *Diario* than when, soon after they had sailed out of Monterey for San Blas, he wrote:

> Don Juan Pérez, the second captain, died at six in the morning [2 November] of typhus, after an illness of nine days. . . . At eight o'clock [3 November] mass *de cuerpo presente* was celebrated, and a sailor's burial was given to the body of Don Juan Pérez, second captain and standard bearer, a salvo of muskets and cannon being fired.[3]

Hezeta makes no mention of this event in his *Diario*, nor had he recorded other such burials at sea of which both Sierra and Campa Cos speak. Whatever the reasons for this, the sea had finally claimed this veteran mariner, whose cautious advice Don Bruno had been so reluctant to heed.

# FOR HONOR AND COUNTRY
## APPENDICES

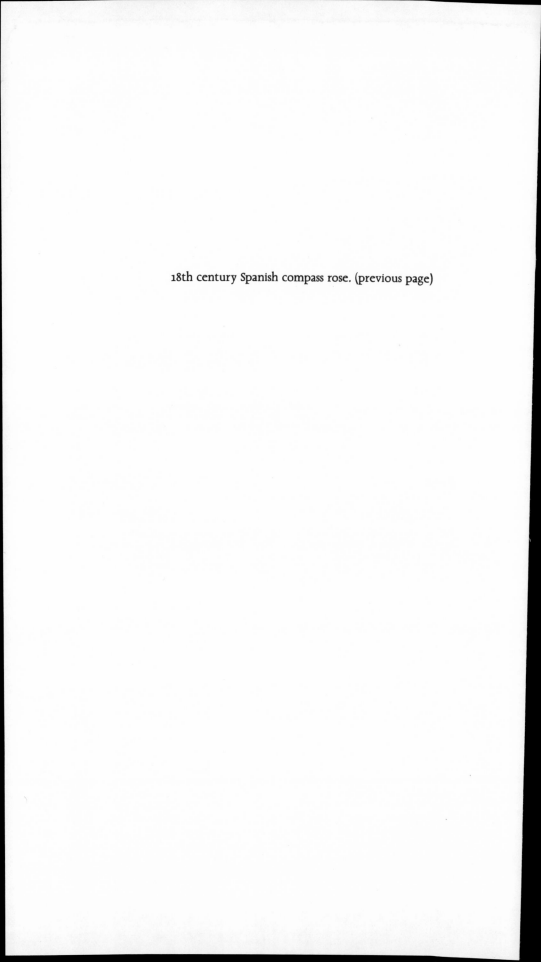

18th century Spanish compass rose. (previous page)

# APPENDIX 1:

## HOW HEZETA NAVIGATED

When Columbus embarked on his "Enterprise of the Indies" in 1492,[1] he crossed the Atlantic with navigational equipment no more elaborate than a magnetic compass, sounding leads, a quadrant and an astrolabe—the last two of which he seldom used. The success of that famous voyage owed little to the science of celestial navigation, then in its infancy. As Samuel Eliot Morison has written, Columbus was "to all intents and purposes . . . a dead-reckoning navigator pure and simple."[2]

By Hezeta's day, navigation methods and equipment had improved, but not as much as might have been expected considering that over two-and-one-half centuries had elapsed since Columbus' epochal voyage of discovery. Invention of the octant in 1730 by John Hadley in England and independently by Thomas Godfrey in America,[3] gave 18th-century mariners a fairly reliable means of determining latitude (position north or south of the equator). A similar advance, however, in solving the problem of longitude (position east or west of a standard meridian) was slower in coming. The most practical means of calculating longitude at sea—by comparing local time with time at some location of known longitude—requires an accurate and durable chronometer. Such an instrument was not invented until 1765 in England, and it was not in general use until after Cook's third voyage (1776–80). Lunar observation was another way of calculating longitude known to 18th-century astronomers, but this was laborious and required mathematical skills that were seldom possessed by seamen.[4]

There are no indications Hezeta had a chronometer aboard or used lunar observations to calculate his longitude. The only method available to him would have been to record his daily course by compass bearing and estimate the distance he sailed each day based on an estimate of the ship's speed—which is called "dead reckoning." Modern navigators still use it, but they have numerous navigational aids to crosscheck and correct their estimated positions. Once out of sight of land, Hezeta's only way of knowing how far west he had sailed from San Blas (his point of departure) was little better than the method used by Columbus.

Today, no prudent seaman would dream of sailing from Mexico to Vancouver Island without a complete and up-to-date set of nautical charts, yet of these Hezeta had only Bellin's 1766 *Carte Reduite*— a tissue of errors and guesswork for most of the coast north of California. Aside from Juan Pérez's *Diario* of his 1774 voyage, the closest navigational aid aboard the *Santiago* to a *Coast Pilot* was apparently Miguel Venegas' *Noticia de la California*. Probably a more useful guide would have been the standard navigation handbook used by pilots on the Manila-Acapulco run, a volume written by Admiral Don Joseph Gonzales Cabrera Bueno entitled *Navegación especulativa y practica* (Understanding and practice of navigation) and published in Manila in 1734. Pérez seems to have carried a copy of this book on his 1774 voyage,[5] and he may have had it with him in 1775. But Hezeta makes no mention of it in his *Diario*.

There were really only four reliable means by which Don Bruno could navigate the *Santiago*: a magnetic compass for direction; daily observations of the sun at noon (weather permitting) for latitude; a sounding lead to plumb the depths; and lookouts aloft to read the ocean's *señas*.

The compass bearings and wind directions mentioned in Hezeta's *Diario* and logged in its appended Tables are expressed in two differing systems. Occasionally his bearings are given according to a compass rose consisting of 32 points equivalent to 11 1/4 degrees each. Inherited from an earlier seafaring age before degrees came into use, this system regarded direction in terms of eight "winds," *los vientos*: N, NE, E, SE, S, SW, W and NW. These winds were divided into eight "half-winds," *los medios vientos*: NNE, ENE, ESE, SSE, SSW, WSW, WNW and NNW; and they in turn were divided into sixteen "quarter winds," *las cuartas*: N 1/4 NE, NE 1/4 N, NE 1/4 E, E 1/4 NE, E 1/4 SE, SE 1/4 E, SE 1/4 S, S 1/4 SE, S 1/4 SW, SW 1/4 S, SW 1/4 W, W 1/4

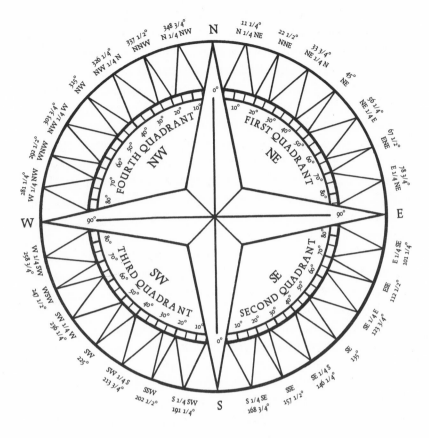

18th Century Spanish Compass Directions

Compass bearings and wind directions logged in Hezeta's *Diario* and appended Tables are expressed in one of two systems illustrated by this compass rose.

One system, stemming from an earlier time before degrees came into use, regarded direction in terms of eight "winds," *los vientos* (N, NE, E, SE, S, SW, W, NW). These were divided into eight "half winds," *los medios vientos* (NNE, ENE, ESE, SSE, SSW, WSW, WNW, NNW); they in turn were divided into sixteen "quarter winds," *las cuartas* (N1/4NE, NE1/4N, NE1/4E, E1/4NE, et cetera). The compass rose was thus divided into 32 points, each equivalent to 11 1/4 degrees.

A second system, of more recent origin and employing degrees, divided the compass rose into four numbered quadrants: First or NE; Second or SE; Third or SW; and Fourth or NW. Each quadrant in turn was divided into 90 degrees, with N and S at zero degrees.

SW, W 1/4 NW, NW 1/4 W, NW 1/4 N and N 1/4 NW. Most of Hezeta's compass bearings, however, are given in a system of more recent origin that did employ degrees. This divided the compass rose into four numbered quadrants: First or NE; Second or SE; Third or SW; and Fourth or NW. Each quadrant in turn was divided into 90 degrees, with N and S at zero degrees. Thus, a bearing equivalent to NE was written "45° of the First Quadrant."

Today, the compass variation or difference between magnetic and true north at San Blas is somewhat over 9°E. When the *Santiago* slipped out of that harbor in 1775, however, Hezeta logged it at only 4 1/2°E. When he was off Vancouver Island, his recorded compass variation reached a maximum of 19°E in an area where modern charts show it 22 1/2°E. This is no indication, however, that Hezeta had some special problem with compass variation. The differences between the variations he observed and those of today are no doubt the result of changes that have occurred in the magnetic pole over two centuries.

Henry R. Wagner believed that Hezeta's observations of latitude involved a fairly consistent error of three or four minutes in excess.[6] A comparison of the latitudes logged in his tables with actual latitudes of known locations shows, however, that the errors were not as consistent as Wagner thought. Of 14 locations checked (opposite) only four were in excess by Wagner's "consistent" three or four minutes. All but four of the observations were within five minutes plus or minus of their actual values. The largest error was ten minutes too low, and the smallest, within one minute. Considering the changeable and adverse conditions under which these observations must have been made, it is not surprising that they vary as they do. They may in fact be regarded as reasonably accurate for the times and circumstances.[7]

Hezeta frequently mentions in his *Diario* taking soundings, and there is no doubt he considered this an important source of navigational information. As he ran close in along uncharted coasts, soundings were vital to avoid running aground, and (as he wrote in his *Diario* in mid-August) it "affirms to the navigator how close he is to land." At least one significant discovery is directly attributable to his diligent use of the sounding lead—the extensive offshore banks along the central Oregon coast, one of which still bears the name

## COMPARISON OF OBSERVED AND ACTUAL LATITUDES
### Voyage of the *Santiago*, 1775

| Location | Hezeta | Actual | Error |
|---|---|---|---|
| Isla Isabela | 21°49' N | 21°52' N | −03' |
| Isla Socorro | 18°50' | 18°46' | +04' |
| Trinidad Harbor | 41°06' | 41°03' | +03' |
| Point Grenville | 47°23' | 47°18' | +05' |
| Victoria Peak | 50°00' | 50°03' | −03' |
| The Golden Hinde | 49°30' | 49°40' | −10' |
| Bodelteh Islands | 48°04' | 48°10' | −06' |
| James Island | 47°58' | 47°54' | +04' |
| Cape Falcon | 45°43' | 45°46' | −03' |
| Three Arch Rocks | 45°30' | 45°28' | +02' |
| Cape Blanco | 42°58' | 42°50' | +08' |
| Sisters Rocks | 42°36' | 42°36' | 00' |
| Punta Gorda | 40°07' | 40°15' | −08' |
| Monterey Harbor | 36°45' | 36°41' | +04' |

of its discoverer. References to soundings are also useful in reconstructing the expedition's track.

Based on remarks recorded while the expedition was at Trinidad Harbor, Hezeta was clearly familiar with the signs used by the Manila galleon pilots to navigate off the North American coast. These were forms of sea life known to occur at definite distances out, which when sighted were an indication of how far one was from the coast. The system, as Hezeta explained it, worked as follows:

| Signs | Leagues from Coast |
|---|---|
| *Aguas malas* (jelly fish) | over 100 |
| *Porras* (kelp) | 70 |
| *Centenares* (birds—Common Murre?) | 40 |
| Puffins (birds) | 5 to 6 |

It was seldom that Don Bruno took unnecessary risks, although his attempt to run the channel between Blanco and Orford reefs on the southern Oregon coast was daring. Apparently his sounding lead that time was stowed, for it was only his vigilant lookout aloft

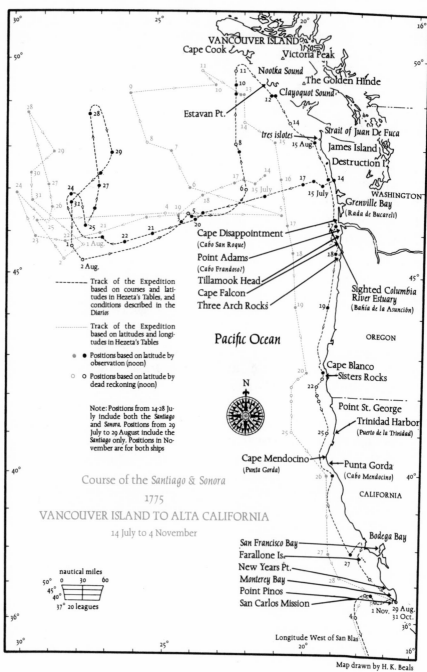

Track of the Expedition based on courses and latitudes in Hezeta's Tables, and conditions described in the Diarios

Track of the Expedition based on latitudes and longitudes in Hezeta's Tables

● Positions based on latitude by observation (noon)

○ Positions based on latitude by dead reckoning (noon)

Note: Positions from 14-28 July include both the *Santiago* and *Sonora*. Positions from 29 July to 29 August include the *Santiago* only. Positions in November are for both ships

Course of the *Santiago* & *Sonora*

1775

VANCOUVER ISLAND TO ALTA CALIFORNIA

14 July to 4 November

nautical miles

0    30    60

20 leagues

Pacific Ocean

N

VANCOUVER ISLAND
Cape Cook
Victoria Peak
Nootka Sound
The Golden Hinde
Clayoquot Sound
Estavan Pt.
tres islotes
15 Aug.
Strait of Juan De Fuca
James Island
Destruction I.
WASHINGTON
Grenville Bay
(Rada de Bucareli)
Cape Disappointment
(Cabo San Roque)
Point Adams
(Cabo Frandoso?)
Tillamook Head
Cape Falcon
Three Arch Rocks
Sighted Columbia
River Estuary
(Bahía de la Asunción)
OREGON
Cape Blanco
Sisters Rocks
Point St. George
Trinidad Harbor
(Puerto de la Trinidad)
Cape Mendocino
(Punta Gorda)
Punta Gorda
(Cabo Mendocino)
CALIFORNIA
Bodega Bay
San Francisco Bay
Farallone Is.
New Years Pt.
Monterey Bay
Point Pinos
San Carlos Mission
1 Nov.    29 Aug.
31 Oct.

Longitude West of San Blas

Map drawn by H. K. Beals

108

who saved the day by warning of the submerged rocks toward which the *Santiago* was headed. His decision not to cross the Columbia River bar on 17 August has been criticized as overly cautious. Yet it is doubtful if many another captain, under the same circumstances, would have done otherwise. With the advantage of hindsight, of course, we know how treacherous such a crossing could have been; Hezeta had only his instincts as a seaman to tell him that this was no maneuver to be attempted by a crew in so weakened a condition.

There are many obstacles to reconstructing an accurate track of the *Santiago's* 1775 voyage. For one thing, we cannot be certain of the length of Hezeta's league. It can only be supposed that it was roughly comparable to the modern marine league of three nautical miles (or three minutes of latitude).[8] A far more serious difficulty stems from Hezeta's lack of a chronometer, for his longitude calculations sometimes suffered from major error. This is not to say his longitude estimates were always so wrong. Hezeta's longitude for Trinidad, for example, was about 28 minutes too far west—not an unreasonable error for the method he employed. Apparently when conditions were favorable his dead-reckoning positions were not seriously off the mark.

Sometime between the 22nd and 29th of June, however, a major error in longitude developed as the expedition stood to the west—

---

The first map of the Northwest Coast (following page) based on the discoveries of the Second Bucareli expedition. In addition to showing the *Sonora's* discoveries in southeastern Alaska, the map notes the *entrada* (Columbia River) discovered by Hezeta at 46[°]N latitude, *Cabo de las Diligencias* (Cape Blanco), Trinidad Harbor and nearby *Río de las Tórtolas*, as well as such other localities mentioned in the Hezeta *Diario* as *Rada de Bucareli* (Grenville Bay) and *Las Tres Marías* (Three Arch Rocks). The map's inscription reads:

Small-scale map of the coasts and waters north of California prepared from the observations and surveys made by second lieutenant Don Juan Francisco de la Bodega y Quadra, commander of the schooner *Sonora*, and by pilot Don Francisco Antonio Maurelle, on the voyage of discoveries on the said coasts and waters, which was ordered by His Excellency, the Viceroy, Frey Don Antonio María Bucareli y Ursúa, [and which] they made in the year 1775.

(Archivo General de Indias, Sevilla. OHS neg.#49258)

109

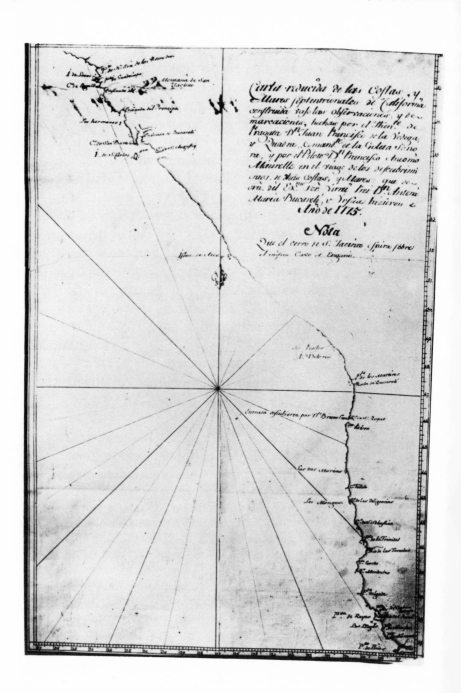

110

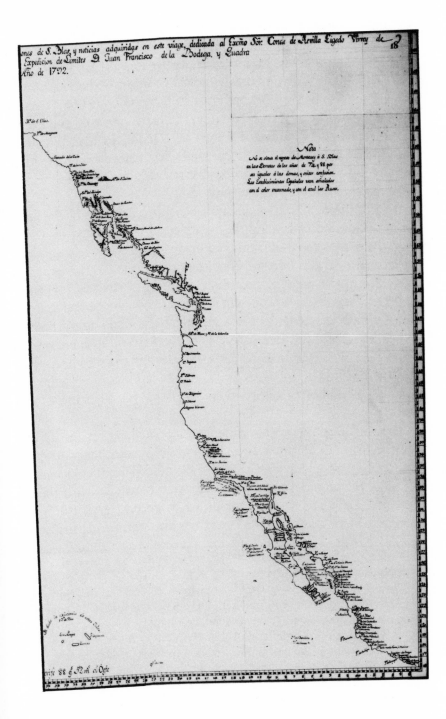

ones de S. Blas, y noticias adquiridas en este viage, dedicada al Exmô Sôr. Conde de Revilla Gigedo Virrey de

Expedicion de Limites D. Juan Francisco de la Bodega, y Quadra

Año de 1792.

18

R.° de S. Elias.

Nota

No se situa el rumbo de Monterey à S. Blas en las Derrotas de los años de 74 y 92 por ser iguales à las demas, y evitar confusion. Los Establecimientos Españoles van señalados con el color encarnado, y con el azul los Rusos.

111

probably because of ocean currents, complicated possibly by the dense fog that enveloped the ships on the 28th. Whatever the reasons, Hezeta appears to have turned north thinking he was some two degrees farther west than his actual position. When he came upon the Washington coast his error in longitude (at Point Grenville) amounted to 2°21' too far west. This error persisted and even got worse in the wind-swept waters off Vancouver Island. It was not until he returned to the vicinity of Cape Blanco on the southern Oregon coast that Hezeta was able to bring his longitude reckoning back into some semblance of reality.

Despite these difficulties, a reasonable approximation of the *Santiago's* track is possible using the navigational data logged by Don Bruno, provided some adjustment is made for his error in longitude by reference to locations and conditions mentioned in the expedition's descriptive accounts. A simple plotting of the *Santiago's* latitudes and longitudes reveals where Hezeta thought he had sailed, but it almost certainly does not represent the ship's actual track. While that is probably unrecoverable in every detail, an approximation is possible by plotting the ship's latitudes and compass bearings, and then adjusting that track to fit known landmarks, soundings, or other conditions mentioned in the *Diario* (*see* adjustment on maps).

To some, Don Bruno's navigational errors might seem a mark of poor seamanship. Still, he was sailing in waters whose silent currents run strong and about which he and his officers knew practically nothing. His problems with longitude were inevitable with these powerful and unseen forces conspiring to deceive even the best dead-reckoning sailor. Coming unexpectedly upon a coast that was

---

Map (previous page) in the collections of the Oregon Historical Society Research Library prepared by Juan Francisco de la Bodega y Quadra in 1792, showing the progress made in charting the North American west coast compared with the fanciful 1726 map of the same coast in Swift's *Gulliver's Travels*. The inscription reads:

Map of the discoveries made on the NW coast of North America by the ships of San Blas, and information acquired on this voyage, dedicated to His Excellency, Conde de Revilla Gigedo, Viceroy of New Spain, by the commander of the boundary expedition, Don Juan Francisco de la Bodega y Quadra in the year 1792.
(Oregon Historical Society. OHS neg.#67563)

supposed to be at least two degrees farther east must have been disconcerting, but as Hezeta himself wrote: "This consideration did not interfere with my making the greatest effort day and night, because I was reflecting on how success can come only through diligence." Of this esteemed quality Hezeta did not lack, and whatever else may be said about his difficulties with longitude, it did not prevent him from bringing his ship and crew back from the unknown northern coasts they had been sent to explore.

# APPENDIX 2:

March 1775 [2]

| Day | Courses by Dead Reckoning | Quad-rant | Distance [3] Sailed | Latitude by Dead Reckoning | Hemi-sphere | Latitude by Obser-vation |
|---|---|---|---|---|---|---|
| [ 1] | | | | | | |
| [ 2] | | | | | | |
| [ 3] | | | | | | |
| [ 4] | | | | | | |
| [ 5] | | | | | | |
| [ 6] | | | | | | |
| [ 7] | | | | | | |
| [ 8] | | | | | | |
| [ 9] | | | | | | |
| [10] | | | | | | |
| [11] | | | | | | |
| [12] | | | | | | |
| [13] | | | | | | |
| [14] | | | | | | |
| [15] | | | | | | |
| 16 | Departure from San Blas, situated at Latitude .... | | | | | 21° 24′ |
| [17] | | | | | | |
| [18] | | | | | | |
| [19] | | | | | | |
| [20] | | | | | | |
| [21] | | | | | | |
| [22] | | | | | | |
| [23] | | | | | | |
| 24 | Sighting of Isla María ....................................................... | | | | | 21° 13′ |
| 25 | 46° 30′ | 3rd | 53–0½ | 20° 35′ | N | 20° 35′ |
| 26 | 70° 30′ | ″ | 61–0½ | 20° 15′ | ″ | 20° 10′ |
| 27 | 74° 00′ | ″ | 67–0½ | 19° 15′ | ″ | 19° 49′ |
| 28 | 47° 00′ | ″ | 35–0⅓ | 19° 25′ | ″ | 19° 27′ |
| 29 | 81° 15′ | ″ | 20–00 | 19° 22′ | ″ | 19° 04′ |
| 30 | 78° 00′ | ″ | 36–0½ | 18° 52′ | ″ | 18° 44′ |
| 31 | 00° 00′ | ″ | 00–00 | 18° 33′ | ″ | 18° 30′ |

[· ·] Indicates where manuscript copy is doubtful or illegible.

114

# HEZETA'S NAVIGATION TABLES[1]

| Cor-rected Courses | Quad-rant | Cor-rected[3] Distance | Longitude W of San Blas | Varia-tions NE | Winds from/to |
|---|---|---|---|---|---|
| | | | 00° 00′ | 4½° | |
| | | | 1° 20′ | | |
| 46° 30′ | 3rd | 53–½ | 1° 58′ | 5° | NW to N |
| 67° 30′ | " | 64–⅓ | 2° 2′ | " | Same |
| 74° 00′ | " | 67–½ | 4° 10′ | " | N to NNW |
| 47° | " | 35–⅓ | 4° 40′ | 5¼° | NW to NNW |
| 44° 10′ | " | 47–0 | 5° 07′ | " | N¼ NW |
| 57° 40′ | " | 41–½ | 5° 37′ | " | N to NW |
| 00° 00′ | South | 3–0 | 5° 37′ | 5½° | Calm |

115

April 1775

| Day | Courses by Dead Reckoning | Quad-rant | Distance[3] Sailed | Latitude by Dead Reckoning | Hemi-sphere | Latitude by Obser-vation |
|---|---|---|---|---|---|---|
| 1 | 22° 30′ | 4th | 03 | 18° 36′ | N | 18° 33′ |
| 2 | 78° 45′ | " | 10–⅓ | 18° 36′ | " | 18° 33′ |
| 3 | 40° 00′ | 1st | 31–½ | 18° 56′ | " | 18° 48′ |
| 4 | 72° 00′ | 3rd | 40–½ | 18° 36′ | " | 18° 30′ |
| 5 | 80° 10′ | " | 28–⅓ | 18° 25′ | " | 18° 16′ |
| 6 | 76° 15′ | " | 50–⅓ | 18° 02′ | " | 17° 48′ |
| 7 | 90° 00′ | " | 60–½ | 17° 45′ | " | 17° 44′ |
| 8 | 89° 00′ | 3rd | 50–0 | 17° 42′ | " | 17° 42′ |
| 9 | 89° 00′ | 4th | 51–½ | 17° 43′ | " | 17° 43′ |
| 10 | 86° 00′ | 3rd | 40–½ | 17° 42′ | " | 17° 35′ |
| 11 | 66° 10′ | 4th | 34–½ | 17° 47′ | " | 17° 47′ |
| 12 | 65° 00′ | " | 38–⅓ | 17° 54′ | " | 17° 44′ |
| 13 | 81° 10′ | " | 31–½ | 17° 49′ | " | 17° 44′ |
| 14 | 73° 40′ | " | 43–0 | 17° 55′ | " | 17° 47′ |
| 15 | 55° 00′ | " | 70–0 | 18° 28′ | " | 18° 20′ |
| 16 | 43° 00′ | " | 66–½ | 19° 6′ | " | |
| 17 | 52° 00′ | " | 73–½ | 19° 31′ | " | 19° 50′ |
| 18 | 48° 10′ | " | 64–0 | 20° 53′ | " | 20° 19′ |
| 19 | 54° 50′ | " | 41–0 | 20° 42′ | " | 20° 37′ |
| 20 | 55° 00′ | " | 27–½ | 20° 53′ | " | |
| 21 | 64° 10′ | " | 34–0 | 21° 08′ | " | |
| 22 | 74° 10′ | " | 37–⅔ | 21° 26′ | " | 21° 04′ |
| 23 | 61° 30′ | " | 34–⅓ | 21° 24′ | " | 21° 21′ |
| 24 | 57° 45′ | " | 63–0 | 21° 55′ | " | 21° 48′ |
| 25 | 52° 00′ | " | 73–0 | 22° 31′ | " | 22° 31′ |
| 26 | 51° 30′ | " | 76–½ | 23° 20′ | " | 23° 21′ |
| 27 | 41° 40′ | " | 72–⅓ | 24° 07′ | " | 24° 12′ |
| 28 | 40° 45′ | " | 47–0 | 24° 48′ | " | 24° 49′ |
| 29 | 55° 45′ | " | 62–⅔ | 25° 24′ | " | 25° 47′ |
| 30 | 44° 30′ | " | 67–0 | 26° 03′ | " | 25° 50′ |

| Corrected Courses | Quadrant | Corrected[3] Distance | Longitude W of San Blas | Variations NE | Winds from/to |
|---|---|---|---|---|---|
| 00° 00′ | W | 00–½ | 5° 37′ | 5½° | Calm |
| 90° 00′ | W | 11–½ | 5° 48′ | " | W |
| 36° 30′ | 3rd | 25–0 | 5° 27′ | " | E to the 3rd quadrant |
| 61° 30′ | 3rd | 43–0 | 6° 04′ | " | N to NNW |
| 60° 15′ | " | 30–0 | 6° 30′ | 5¾° | N to NW |
| 62° 50′ | " | 54–0 | 7° 20′ | " | NNW to NNE |
| 88° 00′ | " | 60–0 | 8° 19′ | " | N to NNE |
| 88° 00′ | " | 50–0 | 9° 06′ | " | N to NNW |
| 88° 00′ | 4th | 51–½ | 10° 00′ | " | NNW to NNE |
| 72° 00′ | 3rd | 44–½ | 10° 38′ | " | N to NNE |
| 84° 40′ | 4th | 32–⅓ | 11° 10′ | " | " |
| 81° 10′ | " | 38–½ | 11° 52′ | " | N to NW |
| 90° 00′ | W | 30–00 | 12° 13′ | " | NW to NE |
| 86° 00′ | 4th | 42–⅔ | 13° 17′ | " | N to NE |
| 62° 10′ | " | 71–⅓ | 14° 03′ | " | NNW to NE |
| | " | | 14° 51′ | " | NE |
| | " | | 15° 52′ | " | NE to NW |
| 58° 50′ | " | 56–½ | 16° 43′ | " | NE to NNE |
| 61° 30′ | " | 37–⅓ | 17° 18′ | " | NNW to N |
| | " | | 17° 41′ | " | N to NE |
| | " | | 18° 15′ | " | NW to NE |
| 84° 50′ | " | 84–50 | 19° 00′ | " | " |
| 65° 40′ | " | 42–⅓ | 19° 41′ | " | NNE |
| 65° 45′ | " | 60–½ | 20° 40′ | " | NE |
| | " | | 21° 34′ | " | " |
| | " | | 22° 39′ | " | NE to ESE |
| 31° 10′ | " | 66–½ | 23° 25′ | " | NE to N |
| | " | | 24° 00′ | " | ENE to N |
| 65° 30′ | 4th | 60–⅓-0 | 24° 59′ | 6 | N to NE |
| 45° 30′ | " | [··] ⅓ | 25° 50′ | " | NE to N |

May 1775

| Day | Courses by Dead Reckoning | Quad-rant | Distance³ Sailed | Latitude by Dead Reckoning | Hemi-sphere | Latitude by Obser-vation |
|---|---|---|---|---|---|---|
| 1 | 51° 10′ | 4th | 51–½ | 26° 29′ | N | 26° 31′ |
| 2 | 38° 30′ | ″ | 12–½ | 26° 44′ | ″ | 26° 44′ |
| 3 | 46° 15′ | ″ | 16–½ | 26° 56′ | ″ | 26° 50′ |
| 4 | 40° 20′ | ″ | 64–⅔ | 27° 40′ | ″ | 27° 38′ |
| 5 | 38° 10′ | ″ | 76–0 | 28° 38′ | ″ | 28° 38′ |
| 6 | 46° 00′ | ″ | 76–½ | 29° 29′ | ″ | 00° 00′ |
| 7 | 52° 50′ | ″ | 64–⅔ | 39° 09′ | ″ | 00° 00′ |
| 8 | 73° 00′ | ″ | 36–0 | 30° 19′ | ″ | 00° 00′ |
| 9 | 67° 30′ | ″ | 44–0 | 30° 36′ | ″ | 00° 46′ |
| 10 | 40° 50′ | ″ | 44–½ | 31° 18′ | ″ | 00° 00′ |
| 11 | 29° 10′ | ″ | 63–0 | 32° 12′ | ″ | 32° 11′ |
| 12 | 05° 50′ | 1st | 63–½ | 33° 14′ | ″ | 33° 15′ |
| 13 | 46° 10′ | ″ | 60–0 | 33° 57′ | ″ | 34° 03′ |
| 14 | 45° 00′ | ″ | 58–0 | 34° 29′ | ″ | 34° 34′ |
| 15 | 71° 50′ | 2nd | 33–0 | 34° 26′ | ″ | 34° 30′ |
| 16 | 71° 30′ | 4th | 51–½ | 34° 46′ | ″ | 34° 54′ |
| 17 | 78° 40′ | 3rd | 14–0 | 34° 15′ | ″ | 34° 50′ |
| 18 | 77° 00′ | 2nd | 04–0 | 34° 49′ | ″ | 34° 50′ |
| 19 | 36° 10′ | 1st | 70–½ | 35° 45′ | ″ | 35° 45′ |
| 20 | 35° 40′ | ″ | 101–½ | 36° 42′ | ″ | 36° 45′ |
| 21 | 64° 40′ | ″ | 49–½ | 37° 06′ | ″ | 35° 01′ |
| 22 | 46° 00′ | 4th | 60–0 | 37° 42′ | ″ | 37° 47′ |
| 23 | 60° 10′ | ″ | 47–½ | 38° 09′ | ″ | 38° 08′ |
| 24 | 42° 00′ | 2nd | 27–0 | 37° 48′ | ″ | 37° 46′ |
| 25 | 02° 10′ | ″ | 16–⅔ | 37° 29′ | ″ | 37° 26′ |
| 26 | 50° 00′ | ″ | 18–½ | 37° 14′ | ″ | 37° 11′ |
| 27 | 73° 20′ | 3rd | 18–0 | 37° 06′ | ″ | |
| 28 | 61° 50′ | 1st | 9–0 | 37° 10′ | ″ | |
| 29 | 43° 40′ | ″ | 52–⅔ | 37° 47′ | ″ | 37° 25′ |
| 30 | 63° 00′ | ″ | 49–0 | 37° 47′ | ″ | 37° 44′ |
| 31 | 69° 00′ | ″ | 39–0 | 37° 48′ | ″ | |

| Corrected Courses | Quadrant | Corrected[3] Distance | Longitude W of San Blas | Variations NE | Winds from/to |
|---|---|---|---|---|---|
| 00° 00′ | ″ | 00–00 | 26° 32′ | 6½° | NE to N |
| 00° 00′ | ″ | 00–00 | 26° 12′ | ″ | NNE to E |
| 64° 15′ | 4th | 12–00 | 26° 56′ | ″ | NE |
| 00° 00′ | ″ | 00–00 | 27° 42′ | ″ | Same |
| 00° 00′ | ″ | 00–00 | 28° 36′ | 7° | NNE to NE |
| 00° 00′ | ″ | 00–00 | 28° 39′ | ″ | N to NE |
| 00° 00′ | ″ | 00–00 | 29° 38′ | ″ | NNW to NNE |
| 00° 00′ | ″ | 00–00 | 30° 18′ | 7½° | Same |
| 58° 00′ | ″ | 43–00 | 31° 05′ | ″ | N to NE |
| 00° 00′ | ″ | 00–00 | 31° 40′ | ″ | NE to E |
| 00° 00′ | ″ | 00–00 | 32° 14′ | 8° | E to SE |
| 00° 00′ | ″ | 00–00 | 32° 09′ | ″ | SSE to E |
| 42° 30′ | 1st | 64–½ | 31° 17′ | ″ | S |
| 57° 50′ | ″ | 61–½ | 30° 14′ | ″ | NE to SSE |
| 80° 00′ | 2nd | 32–0 | 29° 36′ | ″ | NNE |
| 64° 00′ | 4th | 56–0 | 30° 30′ | 8½° | NNW to NE |
| | ″ | | 30° 26′ | ″ | NE to SE |
| | ″ | | 30° 41′ | | SE |
| | ″ | | 29° 51′ | | SSE |
| 54° 40′ | 1st | 104–0 | 28° 06′ | 9° | Varied |
| 70° 30′ | ″ | 48–½ | 27° 10′ | ″ | NE |
| 44° 15′ | 4th | 62–⅔ | 28° 05′ | ″ | N to NE |
| | ″ | 00–00 | 28° 58′ | ″ | N to NNE |
| | ″ | | 28° 35′ | ″ | NNE |
| | ″ | | 28° 34′ | 9° | NNE to ESE |
| 43° 00′ | 2nd | 21–00 | 28° 15′ | | N ¼ NE |
| | ″ | | 28° 37′ | | NW to SW |
| | ″ | | 28° 28′ | | S to W |
| 68° 10′ | 1st | 40–½ | 27° 40′ | | NNW to WNW |
| | ″ | | 26° 40′ | 10° | NW to SW |
| | ″ | | 26° 00′ | | Same |

June 1775

| Day | Courses by Dead Reckoning | Quad- rant | Distance[3] Sailed | Latitude by Dead Reckoning | Hemi- sphere | Latitude by Obser- vation |
|---|---|---|---|---|---|---|
| 1 | 39° 15′ | 1st | 28–½ | 38° 20′ | N | 38° 14′ |
| 2 | 30° 30′ | " | 56–½ | 39° 02′ | " | 00° 00′ |
| 3 | 45° 30′ | " | 63–0 | 39° 46′ | " | 39° 51′ |
| 4 | 51° 00′ | " | 40–½ | 40° 13′ | " | 00° 00′ |
| 5 | 36° 30′ | " | 72–0 | 41° 11′ | " | 41° 22′ |
| 6 | 71° 30′ | " | 85–⅓ | 41° 41′ | " | 41° 37′ |
| 7 | 73° 20′ | " | 44–0 | 41° 49′ | " | 41° 30′ |
| 8 | 51° 00′ | " | 26–0 | 41° 39′ | " | 41° 43′ |
| 9 | 22° 30′ | 2nd | 07–0 | 41° 32′ | " | 41° 14′ |
| 10 | Anchored in Trinidad, located at ....................... | | | | | 41° 06′ |
| [11] | | | | | | |
| [12] | | | | | | |
| [13] | | | | | | |
| [14] | | | | | | |
| [15] | | | | | | |
| [16] | | | | | | |
| [17] | | | | | | |
| [18] | | | | | | |
| [19] | | | | | | |
| 20 | Departure from Trinidad, sighting | | | | N | 40° 59′ |
| 21 | 87° ½′ | 4th | 15–½ | 40° 59′ | N | 40° 53′ |
| 22 | 64° 00′ | 3rd | 63–⅔ | 40° 25′ | " | 40° 08′ |
| 23 | 81° 30′ | " | 36–0 | 40° 02′ | " | 40° 00′ |
| 24 | 76° 10′ | " | 63–½ | 39° 45′ | " | 00° 00′ |
| 25 | 67° 30′ | " | 54–0 | 39° 25′ | " | 39° 26′ |
| 26 | 88° 00′ | " | 72–½ | 39° 22′ | " | 39° 21′ |
| 27 | 87° 00′ | 4th | 46–0 | 39° 51′ | " | 39° 22′ |
| 28 | 13° 30′ | 1st | 32–0 | 39° 49′ | " | 00° 00′ |
| 29 | 81° 00′ | 3rd | 12–½ | 39° 24′ | " | 00° 00′ |
| 30 | 22° 30′ | 1st | 40–00 | 40° 26′ | " | 40° 16′ |

| Cor-rected Courses | Quad-rant | Cor-rected[3] Distance | Longitude W of San Blas | Varia-tions NE | Winds from/to |
|---|---|---|---|---|---|
| 50° 10' | 1st | 23–½ | 25° 36' | 10½° | SE to SW |
| 00° 00' | | 56–0 | 24° 59' | 11° | NE to SE |
| 43° ⅔' | " | 65–⅔ | 24° 02' | 11½° | S to SW |
| 00° 00' | " | 90–0 | 23° 49' | 12¾° | SE to SSE |
| 32° 00' | " | 87–½ | 22° 22' | 14½° | WSW to SW |
| 80° 15' | " | 86–½ | 20° 40' | | SW to WSW |
| 80° 30' | " | 43–0 | 19° 43' | 13½° | N to NW |
| 55° 30' | 2nd | 23–0 | 19° 17' | | |
| 00° 10' | " | 24–1 | 29° 17' | 14° | |
| | | | 19° 17' | | |
| | " | | 19° 04' | 00 | |
| 67° 00' | 3rd | 16–½ | 19° 30' | 15° | |
| 50° 00' | " | 72– | 20° 56' | 00 | |
| 00° 00' | " | 00– | 21° 40' | 00 | |
| 00° 00' | " | 00– | 22° 59' | 00 | |
| 00° 00' | " | 00– | 24° 03' | 00 | |
| 00° 00' | W | 00– | 25° 35' | 00 | |
| 00° 00' | " | 00– | 26° 36' | 14° | |
| 00° 00' | " | 00– | 26° 42' | 00 | |
| 00° 00' | " | 00– | 26° 57' | 00 | |
| 29° 30' | 1st | 31–½ | 26° 26' | 00 | |

July 1775

| Day | Courses by Dead Reckoning | Quad-rant | Distance[3] Sailed | Latitude by Dead Reckoning | Hemi-sphere | Latitude by Obser-vation | |
|---|---|---|---|---|---|---|---|
| 1 | 10° 50′ | 1st | 47−½ | 45° 17′ | N | 41° 01′ | |
| 2 | 19° 00′ | 4th | 80−⅔ | 42° 17′ | " | 42° 15′ | |
| 3 | 00° 00′ | N | 70− | 43° 25′ | " | | |
| 4 | 13° 50′ | 1st | 58−½ | 44° 21′ | " | | |
| 5 | 28° 30′ | " | 30−½ | 44° 27′ | " | | |
| 6 | 19° 00′ | " | 50− | 45° 14′ | " | | |
| 7 | 13° 30′ | 4th | 57−½ | 46° 10′ | " | | |
| 8 | 20° 30′ | 1st | 52− | 46° 39′ | " | 47° 03′ | |
| 9 | 52° 20′ | " | 68−¼ | 47° 44′ | " | 47° 37′ | |
| 10 | 74° 10′ | " | 29−½ | 47° 45′ | " | 47° 35′ | |
| 11 | 43° 20′ | 1st | 79− | 48° 32′ | " | 48° 26′ | |
| 12 | 32° 30′ | 2nd | 29−⅔ | 48° 01′ | " | 47° 39′ | |
| 13 | 77° 20′ | 1st | 09− | 47° 41′ | " | 47° 28′ | |
| 14 | 69° 30′ | 2nd | 11−⅓ | 47° 23′ | " | 47° 23′ | |
| 15 | 85° 30′ | 3rd | 14− | 47° 23′ | " | 47° 07′ | |
| 16 | 54° 00′ | 4th | 23− | 47° 20′ | " | 47° 13′ | |
| 17 | 73° 30′ | " | 14− | 47° 17′ | " | 47° 09′ | |
| 18 | 83° 00′ | 3rd | 49− | 47° 04′ | " | 46° 52′ | |
| 19 | 65° 00′ | 3rd | 42− | 46° 34′ | " | 46° 26′ | |
| 20 | 79° 00′ | 3rd | 42− | 46° 18′ | " | 46° 18′ | |
| 21 | 80° 10′ | 3rd | 67−½ | 46° 06′ | " | 45° 57′ | |
| 22 | 82° 00′ | 3rd | 51− | 45° 50′ | " | 45° 44′ | |
| 23 | 90° 00′ | E | 46− | 45° 44′ | " | 45° 51′ | |
| 24 | 72° 30′ | 4th | 35− | 45° 51′ | " | 46° 54′ | |
| 25 | 34° 30′ | 1st | 16− | 46° 04′ | " | 46° 09′ | |
| 26 | 11° 15′ | 1st | 25−½ | 46° 34′ | " | 46° 32′ | |
| 27 | 08° 10′ | 4th | 34−½ | 47° 06′ | " | 47° 05′ | |
| 28 | 17° 00′ | 1st | 41−⅔ | 47° 43′ | " | 48° 44′ | |
| 29 | 56° 15′ | 1st | 45−½ | 48° 10′ | " | 47° 50′ | |
| 30 | 47° 30′ | 3rd | 44− | 47° 20′ | " | 47° 21′ | |
| 31 | 00° 00′ | 3rd | 38− | 46° 42′ | " | 46° 42′ | |

122

| Cor-<br>rected<br>Courses | Quad-<br>rant | Cor-<br>rected[3]<br>Distance | Longitude<br>W of<br>San Blas | Varia-<br>tions<br>NE | Winds from/to |
|---|---|---|---|---|---|
| | " | " | 26° 14′ | 14° | SW |
| | " | " | 26° 49′ | " | " |
| | " | " | 26° 50′ | " | WSW |
| | " | " | 26° 30′ | " | SW ¼ W |
| | " | " | 26° 10′ | " | W |
| | " | " | 25° 47′ | " | W ¼ NW |
| | " | " | 26° 06′ | " | W ¼ SW |
| 18° 30′ | 1st | 56– | 25° 40′ | 17° | W to NW |
| 56° 50′ | 2nd | 64–½ | 24° 20′ | " | NW to WNW |
| 86° 00′ | 2nd | 28–0 | 23° 38′ | " | WNW |
| 46° 30′ | 1st | 74–½ | 22° 17′ | " | NW to W |
| 18° 40′ | 2nd | 49–⅓ | 21° 53′ | " | Almost calm |
| 49° 30′ | 2nd | 17–0 | 21° 34′ | " | NW |
| | " | " | 21° 19′ | " | NW |
| 40° 00′ | 3rd | 22–⅓ | 21° 40′ | 17° 30′ | NW |
| 69° 30′ | 4th | 17–0 | 22° 03′ | " | WSW |
| 72° 30′ | 3rd | 13–0 | 22° 22′ | " | Calm |
| 70° 50′ | 3rd | 52–0 | 23° 32′ | " | NW |
| 56° 00′ | 3rd | 46–0 | 24° 18′ | " | NW to N |
| | " | " | 25° 29′ | 16° | NNW |
| 73° 00′ | 3rd | 69–0 | 27° 05′ | " | NW to N |
| 75° 30′ | " | 52–⅓ | 28° 18′ | 15° | NNW |
| 85° 10′ | 3rd | 46–¼ | 29° 26′ | " | NNW |
| | " | " | 30° 12′ | " | Variable |
| 25° 10′ | 1st | 20–0 | 29° 59′ | " | Same |
| | " | " | 29° 52′ | " | NW to W |
| | " | " | 29° 59′ | 16° | NW |
| 19° 10′ | 1st | 37– | 29° 41′ | " | " |
| 75° 10′ | 1st | 30–⅓ | 28° 44′ | " | " |
| | " | " | 29° 32′ | " | " |
| | " | " | 29° 32′ | " | " |

August 1775

| Day | Courses by Dead Reckoning | Quad-rant | Distance[3] Sailed | Latitude by Dead Reckoning | Hemi-sphere | Latitude by Obser-vation |
|---|---|---|---|---|---|---|
| 1 | 36° 0′ | 2nd | 98–0 | 45° 40′ | N | |
| 2 | [· · ·] 0′ | ″ | 59–0 | 45° 20′ | ″ | |
| 3 | 67° 0′ | 1st | 48–½ | 45° 42′ | ″ | 46° 12′ |
| 4 | 67° 30′ | | 31–0 | 46° 26′ | ″ | |
| 5 | 70° 0′ | [· · ·] | [· · ·] | 46° 35′ | ″ | 46° 24′ |
| 6 | 11° 0′ | 4th | 41–0 | 47° 00′ | ″ | |
| 7 | 43° | 4th | 42–½ | 47° 09′ | ″ | 47° 54′ |
| 8 | 00° | | 39–½ | 48° [· · ·] | ″ | |
| 9 | [· · ·] | [· · ·] | [· · ·] | | ″ | 49° 11′ |
| 10 | 00° 00′ | N | 12–00 | 49° 23′ | ″ | 49° 23′ |
| 11 | 00° 00′ | N | 17– | 49° 40′ | ″ | 49° [· · ·] |
| 12 | 61° 10′ | 2nd | 68–½ | 49° 9′ | ″ | 49° 10′ |
| 13 | 40° 10′ | 3rd | 41– | 49° 0′ | ″ | 49° 11′ |
| 14 | 00° 00′ | S | 34– | 48° 32′ | ″ | |
| 15 | 55° 30′ | 2nd | [· · ·] | 48° [· · ·] | ″ | 48° 6′ |
| 16 | 50° 30′ | 2nd | 52– | 47° 11′ | ″ | 47° 13′ |
| 17 | 5° 11′ | 2nd | 59–½ | 46° 13′ | ″ | 46° 11′ |
| 18 | 21° 30′ | 2nd | 41–0 | 45° 38′ | ″ | 45° 35′ |
| 19 | 1° | ″ | 82–0 | 44° 14′ | ″ | 44° 13′ |
| 20 | 12° 30′ | ″ | 100– | 42° [· · ·] | ″ | 42° 35′ |
| 21 | 61° 48′ | 3rd | 21–0 | 42° 25′ | ″ | ″ |
| 22 | 39° 0′ | 3rd | 13– | 42° 16′ | ″ | ″ |
| 23 | 00° 00′ | S | 14– | 42° | ″ | ″ |
| 24 | 00° 00′ | S | 50– | 41° 50′ | ″ | ″ |
| 25 | 00° 00′ | S | 50– | 41° | ″ | ″ |
| 26 | 60° 40′ | 2nd | 42– | 40° 40′ | ″ | 39° 58′ |
| 27 | 00° 00′ | S | 34– | 38° 20′ | ″ | 37° 50′ |
| 28 | 86° 30′ | 2nd | 37–48 | 37° 09′ | ″ | |
| 29 | 40° 50′ | ″ | 89– | 36° 45′ | Anchored in | |

124

| Cor-rected Courses | Quad-rant | Cor-rected³ Distance | Longitude W of San Blas | Varia-tions NE | Winds from/to |
|---|---|---|---|---|---|
| | | | 27° 39' | 18° | N ¼ NE |
| | | | 28° 22' | | NNW |
| 39° | 1st | 65-½ | 29° 20' | " | Same |
| | | " | 24° 44' | " | " |
| 00° 0' | E | 41-0 | 20° 44' | " | " |
| " | " | | 23° 55' | 18° | W |
| 30° | 4th | 58-0 | 24° 35' | " | SW to SE |
| " | " | " | 25° 29' | " | SE to E |
| " | | | 26° 01' | 19° | Variable |
| | " | " | 23° 01' | " | WNW |
| " | " | " | 23° 39' | 18° | Calm |
| " | | " | 22° 03' | " | NW |
| " | " | " | 22° 6' | " | " |
| | " | " | 22° 6' | " | " |
| " | " | | 20° 58' | " | " |
| " | | " | 20° 46' | " | " |
| " | " | | 20° 31' | 17° | SE |
| | " | " | [· · ·] 16' | | NW |
| " | | " | 20° 14' | " | " |
| " | " | " | 19° 44' | " | " |
| " | " | " | 20° 09' | " | " |
| " | " | " | 20° 19' | " | [· · ·] |
| " | " | " | 20° 19' | " | Same |
| " | " | " | 20° 19' | " | Same |
| " | " | " | 20° 19' | " | Same |
| 30° 00' | 2nd | 72- | 19° 00' | " | NW |
| 00° 00' | W | [· · ·] | 19° 00' | 16° | NW |
| | | | 18° 35' | | NW |
| Monterey [· · · · · ·] | | | [· · ·] 17' | | NW |

November 1775

| Day | Courses by Dead Reckoning | Quad-rant | Distance[3] Sailed | Latitude by Dead Reckoning | Hemi-sphere | Latitude by Obser-vation |
|---|---|---|---|---|---|---|
| 1 | 40° 30′ | 4th | 08– | 36° 48′ | N | |
| 2 | 46° 00′ | 3rd | 16– | 36° 42′ | " | 36° 42′ |
| 3 | according to sighting | | | 36° 35′ | " | |
| 4 | according to sighting | | | 36° 11′ | " | |
| 5 | 13° 00′ | 2nd | 84– | 34° 45′ | " | |
| 6 | 14° 00′ | 2nd | 111– | 33° 00′ | " | 32° 48′ |
| 7 | 24° 45′ | 2nd | 124– | 30° 54′ | " | 30° 56′ |
| 8 | 25° | 2nd | 103– | 29° 22′ | " | 20° 15′ |
| 9 | 48° | 2nd | 41–½ | 28° 47′ | " | |
| 10 | 48° 15′ | 2nd | 41– | 28° 18′ | " | 27° 50′ |
| 11 | 49° 30′ | 2nd | 58–½ | 27° 11′ | " | 27° 09′ |
| 12 | 53° 00′ | 2nd | 82– | 26° 21′ | " | 26° 11′ |
| 13 | 60° 00′ | 2nd | 105– | 25° 18′ | " | 25° 12′ |
| 14 | 70° 00′ | 2nd | 103– | 24° 36′ | " | 24° 34′ |
| 15 | 77° 40′ | 2nd | 109– | 24° 11′ | " | 24° 01′ |
| 16 | 65° 50′ | 2nd | 86–½ | 23° 26′ | " | 23° 00′ |
| 17 | 67° 30′ | 2nd | 84– | 22° 27′ | " | 22° 25′ |
| 18 | 80° 30′ | 2nd | 88–½ | 22° 15′ | " | 21° 55′ |
| 19 | 85° 10′ | 2nd | 96– | 21° 47′ | " | 21° 40′ |
| 20 | Anchored in the Port of San Blas | | | | " | 21° 30′ |

| Cor-rected Courses | Quad-rant | Cor-rected [3] Distance | Longitude W of San Blas | Varia-tions NE | Winds from/to |
|---|---|---|---|---|---|
| | " | | 17° 24' | 12° | |
| | " | | 17° 39' | | |
| | " | | 17° 48' | | |
| | " | | 18° 02' | 10° 30' | |
| | " | | 17° 37½' | 10° 00' | |
| 46° 00' | 2nd | 121– | 17° 08' | 9° 30' | |
| | " | | 16° 01' | 9° 00' | |
| 24° 00' | 2nd | 110– | 15° 10' | 8° 30' | |
| | " | | 14° 35' | 8° 00' | |
| 36° 00' | 2nd | 71– | 13° 52' | | |
| | " | | 13° 01' | 7° 00' | |
| 48° 00' | 2nd | 89–¼ | 11° 48' | | |
| 57° 00' | 2nd | 110– | 10° 09' | | |
| | " | | 08° 20' | 6° 30' | |
| 73° 00' | 2nd | 112– | 06° 23' | 6° 00' | |
| 52° 10' | 2nd | 100– | 05° 05' | 5° 00' | |
| | " | | 03° 39' | 5° 00' | |
| 77° 00' | 2nd | 92–½ | 02° 04' | | |
| 81° 45' | 2nd | 96– | 00° 22' | 5° 00' | |
| | " | | | 4° 30' | |

127

# GLOSSARY

Arroba.  Spanish unit of weight equivalent to 25 English pounds. It is also the name of a variable unit of liquid volume.

Anclote.  Spanish term translated as "stream anchor," meaning a small anchor used to pull or kedge a ship along by means of winding a rope or cable on to a capstan. It is also called a kedge anchor.

Braza.  Spanish term for fathom. It is equivalent to two varas (Spanish yards) or five-and-one-half English feet. An English fathom is six feet.

Cable.  Spanish term translated as "cable length." In Spanish usage it was a measurement of 120 brazas (660 feet), and in English usage a measurement of 120 fathoms (720 English feet).

Capear or Hacer Capa.  Spanish term or phrase translated as "to lay to," meaning to halt the motion of a ship, usually by turning the bow into the wind and trimming the sails so they act against each other. Also equivalent to the term "to heave to."

Ceñir el Viento.  Spanish phrase translated as "to haul the wind," meaning to sail a ship as close to or as far into the wind as its rigging will permit.

Pie.  Spanish term translated as "foot." In Spanish usage it was a measurement equivalent to 11 English inches.

Pairar or Estar a la Capa.  Spanish term or phrase translated as "to lie to," meaning for a ship to remain comparatively stationary.

Legua.  Spanish term translated as "league." On land it was a measurement in Spanish usage of 5,000 varas or about two-and-two-thirds statute miles. At sea a league is equivalent to three nautical miles or three minutes of latitude in modern usage. Hezeta does not say explicitly which league he intended, but the marine league (or some approximation thereof) seems most likely.

Milla.   Spanish term translated as "mile." In modern usage a nautical mile is equivalent to 6,076 English feet or one minute of latitude. A statute mile is equivalent to 5,280 English feet. While it is more likely Hezeta used this term roughly in equivalence to the nautical mile, the exact value he gave it is uncertain.

Ranchería.   Spanish term for a small Indian settlement, usually implying a group of structures and cultivated plots.

Tuesa.   Spanish unit of length equivalent to two varas or five-and-one-half English feet.

Vara.   Spanish term for yard. It was equivalent to two-and-three-fourths feet or thirty-three inches (English).

Virar.   Spanish term translated as "to tack," "to veer," or "to come about," meaning to change the course of a ship by bringing the bow into the wind and falling off to the opposite side by turning away from the wind. To sail a zigzag course into the wind (beating windward) is called tacking (sp. virada).

# NOTES: INTRODUCTION

1. Swift, *Gulliver's Travels*, pp.122–23.

2. Wagner, *Spanish Voyages to the Northwest Coast of America in the Sixteenth Century*, p.4.

3. Wagner, *Spanish Voyages*, pp.5–6. *See also* Morison, *The European Discovery of America: The Southern Voyages, A.D. 1492–1616*, pp.620–21; López de Gómara (trans. and ed. by Simpson), *Cortés: The Life of the Conqueror by His Secretary* (from the *Istoria de la Conquista de Mexico*), pp.396–98.

4. Wagner, *Spanish Voyages*, p.6.

5. Morison, *European Discovery*, p.620.

6. "The Narrative of Alvar Núñez Cabeza de Vaca," in Hodge and Lewis (eds.), *Spanish Explorers in the Southern United States, 1528–1543*, p.106.

7. *See* Bolton, *Coronado: Knight of Pueblo and Plains*, and "The Narrative of the Expedition of Coronado," by Pedro de Castañeda, in Hodge and Lewis (eds.), *Spanish Explorers*, pp.281–387.

8. Wagner, *Spanish Voyages*, p.8.

9. Wagner, *Spanish Voyages*, p.11. Cortés expressly claimed that Ulloa was dispatched in search of Cíbola. Herbert Bolton (*Coronado*, pp.46–47), however, contends that although Cortés unquestionably sent Ulloa to find the fabulous cities reported by Cabeza de Vaca, it is doubtful if he knew them as "Cíbola"—a name that came into use somewhat later. *See also* López de Gómara, *Cortés*, pp.403–404.

10. Ulloa's narrative and other related documents are found in Wagner, *Spanish Voyages*, pp.15–50.

11. Wagner, *Spanish Voyages*, p.14.

12. Morison, *European Discovery*, pp.623–24.

13. Hodges and Lewis (eds.), *Spanish Explorers*, p.364.

14. Wagner, *Spanish Voyages*, p.59.

15. Henry L. Oak was one of the writers of Bancroft's *History of the Northwest Coast*. *See* vol. 1, p.5.

16. Wagner, *Spanish Voyages*, pp.79–83, 426–30.

17. Wagner, *Spanish Voyages*, p.85.

18. Wagner, *Spanish Voyages*, pp.86–87. For a detailed description of the Chumash, *see* Heizer (ed.), *Handbook of North American Indians*, vol. 8, *California*, pp.505–534.

19. Wagner, *Spanish Voyages*, p.88.

20. Cutter, "Spain and the Oregon Coast," in Vaughan (ed.), *The Western Shore*, pp.32–33.

21. Wagner, *Spanish Voyages*, p.77.

22. Wagner, *Spanish Voyages*, p.89.

23. Wagner points out that depths of 45 fathoms can be found close to shore at Monterey Bay. No other bays along the California coast between the Santa Barbara Channel and 40°N, that could be called a "large *ensenada*," have such depths close to shore. *See* Morison, *European Discovery*, p.630, and Wagner, *Spanish Voyages*, pp.78–79, 89, 335 (n. 104), 336 (n. 106).

24. An alternate version suggests that Cabrillo may have died of a broken leg he suffered in going to the assistance of some of his men in a skirmish with Indians. *See* Wagner, *Spanish Voyages*, p.336 (n. 113), and Holmes, *From New Spain by Sea to the Californias, 1519–1668*, pp.110–11.

25. Wagner, *Spanish Voyages*, p.93.

26. This presumably is a reference to logs or other vegetation seen floating at sea. Wagner notes that from the Eel River (lat. 40°37′N) north there are numerous rivers that discharge such materials into the ocean. *See* Wagner, *Spanish Voyages*, pp.92, 337 (n. 124).

27. Morga, *Sucesos de las Islas Filipinas*, p.306.

28. Details and documents of this voyage are in Wagner, *Spanish Voyages*, pp. 94–124.

29. Schurz, *The Manila Galleon*, pp.238–39, and Morga, *Sucesos*, p.322. *See also* Hezeta Diario, entry for 18 June (*see* "Notes for Hezeta's Diario," notes 27, 28 and 29).

30. This quotation is attributed to historian Padre Casimiro Diaz in Schurz' comprehensive study, *The Manila Galleon*, p.253.

31. Penzer (ed.), *The World Encompassed*, p.48.

32. *See* Hanna, *Lost Harbor: The Controversy over Drake's California Anchorage*, for an impartial and comprehensive examination of the many facets of this debate. Heizer's *Elizabethan California* is another useful survey of the debate, particularly from an anthropological standpoint. Wagner's *Sir Francis Drake's Voyage Around the World* is still the most comprehensive work on Drake's entire circumnavigation, although some of his opinions on its California phase are no longer tenable. The maximum northern latitude reached by the *Golden Hind* on the North American coast has also been a subject of controversy. For the argument that Drake reached Vancouver Island, *see* Bishop, "Drake's Course in the North Pacific," *British Columbia Historical Quarterly*, 3:3; Holmes, "Francis Drake's Course in the North Pacific, 1579," *Geographical Bulletin*, 17.

33. Wagner, *Sir Francis Drake*, pp.347, 349.

34. Wagner, *Spanish Voyages*, p.132. Moya's letter to Philip II appears to have been written after Moya was informed of the urgency of the need to explore the northern coasts by a letter from a Fray Andrés de Aguirre. Aguirre's letter also calls attention to the so-called Armenian Isles, thought to have lain in the North Pacific between Japan and the American coast. *See* Cutter, *The California Coast*, pp.10–17, for the text of Aguirre's letter.

35. Details and documents relating to Gali and his proposal to Viceroy Moya are in Wagner, *Spanish Voyages*, pp.125–38.

36. *See* Wagner, *Spanish Voyages*, p.151–52, and Mathes, *Vizcaino and Spanish Expansion in the Pacific Ocean, 1580–1630*, p.15 (n.19).

37. Details and documents of Unamuno's voyage are in Wagner, *Spanish Voyages*, pp.139–53.

38. *See* Gerhard, *Pirates on the West Coast of New Spain, 1575–1742*, pp.89–94.

39. Gerhard, *Pirates*, pp.94–95.

40. *See* Cook, *Flood Tide of Empire*, pp.10, 24–26.

41. The full text of Michael Lok's account of Fuca's supposed 1592 voyage is given in Cook, *Flood Tide*, pp.539–43.

42. Viceroy Velesco's letter of 6 April 1594, in reply to the Royal Order is in Cutter, *California Coast*, pp.28–29.

43. *See* Wagner, *Spanish Voyages*, p.155; Mathes, *Vizcaino*, p.45.

44. *See* Velasco's letter in Cutter, *California Coast*, p.29.

45. Details and documents of Cermeño's voyage are in Wagner, *Spanish Voyages*, pp.154–67. Much confusion surrounds the use of the name Cabo Mendocino, because early Spanish navigators (such as Cermeño) seem to have applied the name to other northern California headlands than the one that today bears the name Cape Mendocino.

46. Wagner was inclined to think it was Rocky Point because of its lower latitude—he almost always regarded 16th century observations of latitude as being too high—despite the fact that Point St. George better fits the description given in the narrative. *See Spanish Voyages*, pp.157, 369 (n.19), 370 (n.20). This location is close to where the Hezeta expedition made its first landfall in June 1775; *see Hezeta Diario*, entries for 8 and 9 of June.

47. Wagner, *Spanish Voyages*, p.157. It is interesting that when Hezeta entered 180 years later what must have been this same harbor he was not so fearful of its undeniably rocky bottom, making good use of the resources of Puerto de la Trinidad, as he called it. *See Hezeta Diario*, entries from 9 to 19 June.

48. Wagner, *Spanish Voyages*, p.158.

49. Wagner, *Spanish Voyages*, p.157.

50. Morison summarizes the evidence supporting the identification of Drakes Bay as the harbor in which the *Golden Hind* was careened in *European Discovery*, pp. 669–73.

51. *See* "Archaeological Evidence of Sebastián Rodríguez Cermeño's California Visit in 1595," *California Historical Society Quarterly*, 20:4, pp.315–28.

52. *See*, for example, conde de Monterey's letter to Philip II of 29 February 1596, in Cutter, *California Coast*, pp.50–57.

53. Letter of conde de Monterey to Philip II of 26 November 1597 in Cutter, *California Coast*, p.99.

54. Interestingly enough, one of the Drake narratives refers to his northward track as a "Spanish course." *See* Wagner, *Drake's Voyage*, p.274. One explanation of this may be that what was meant by a "Spanish course" was the course taken by the Manila ships outbound from Acapulco which took them directly westward into the Pacific between 10° and 15°N latitude. Drake probably followed such a course for several hundred miles but then veered northward leaving the so-called "Spanish course" in his search for the Strait of Anian. *See* Bishop, "Drake's Course in the North Pacific," *British Columbia Historical Quarterly*, 3:3, p.165.

55. The viceroy wanted nothing to tempt Vizcaíno into going astray before the charting of the outer coast had been accomplished, but he apparently had no objections to an excursion in the gulf for pearls on the return voyage. *See* Mathes, *Vizcaíno*, p.57.

56. Details and documents of Vizcaíno's voyage are in Wagner, *Spanish Voyages*, pp.168–285, and Cutter, *California Coast*, pp.46–117. *See also* Mathes, *Vizcaíno*, pp.54–107.

57. Cutter, *California Coast*, p.109.

58. Fray Antonio de la Ascención's account, in Wagner, *Spanish Voyages*, p.249.

59. Ascención's account, in Wagner, *Spanish Voyages*, p.253.

60. Hezeta remarks about finding what he believed to be this cape. *See* the *Diario* entry for 20 August.

61. Ascención's account, in Wagner, *Spanish Voyages*, p.255.

62. Hezeta searched vainly for this river. See the *Diario* entries for 21 May (under the subtitle Notes) and 20 August.

63. *See* Vizcaíno's letter to Philip III, 23 May 1603, in Cutter, *California Coast*, pp.112–17.

64. Marqués de Montesclaros' letter to Philip III, 4 August 1607, in Wagner, *Spanish Voyages*, p.278. *See* Wagner, *Spanish Voyages*, pp.273–82, for details and documents relating to the project to settle Monterey and Montesclaros' opposition to it.

65. Wagner, *Spanish Voyages*, p.277.

66. *See* Mathes, *Vizcaíno*, pp.108–14.

67. *See* Kelly (ed. and trans.) "The Journal of Fray Martín de Munilla O.F.M.," in *La Austrialia Del Espíritu Santo*, vol. 1, pp.257–70.

68. Schurz, *The Manila Galleon*, p.254.

69. Schurz (*The Manila Galleon*, p.260) says the *Xavier* cleared Manila in 1705, while Cook (*Flood Tide*, pp.34–35, n.38), citing a French source, says it left Manila in January 1707. The beeswax found in northern Tillamook County, Oregon, is described in Stafford, "The Wax of Nehalem Beach," *Oregon Historical Quarterly*, 9:1, pp.24–41. Chinese porcelain shards were excavated in 1959 from the site of an aboriginal house on the Netarts sand spit and reported by Newman in "Tillamook Prehistory and its Relation to the Northwest Coast Culture Area," pp. 30, 59. The shards were originally thought to be 18th century, but subsequent studies suggest they probably are 17th century or even somewhat earlier. Similar shards have also been reported from the Nehalem sand spit and the vicinity of Seaside, Oregon. *See* Beals and Steele, "Chinese Porcelains from Site 35-TI-1, Netarts Sand Spit, Tillamook County, Oregon," *University of Oregon Anthropological Papers*, No. 23. For further discussion of the myths and legends concerning early shipwrecks and castaways on the northern Oregon coast *see* Cook, *Flood Tide*, pp.31–40; Clarke, *Pioneer Days of Oregon History*, vol. 1, pp.155–76.

70. *See* Gerhard, *Pirates on the West Coast of New Spain, 1575–1742*.

71. Golder, *Bering's Voyages*, vol. 1, p.290.

72. Golder, *Bering's Voyages*, vol. 1. pp.1–5, 25–26.

73. Fisher, *Bering's Voyages: Whither and Why*, pp.152–79.

74. See Cook, *Flood Tide of Empire*, pp.41–50, for a more detailed exposition of the influence of Russian activity on the revival of Spanish interest in the north.

75. See Thurman, *The Naval Department of San Blas*, pp.1–72, for details of the founding of the San Blas naval base.

76. See "The Instructions of Viceroy Bucareli to Ensign Juan Pérez," in *California Historical Society Quarterly*, 40:3, pp.237–48.

77. Thurman, *Naval Department*, p.128.

78. Accounts of the 1774 Pérez voyage after it left Monterey, kept by the ship's two chaplains, Fray Tomás de la Peña and Fray Juan Crespi, are in Cutter, *California Coast*, pp.136–278. Pérez's own account is in his unpublished "Continuación del Diario . . . 1774," copies of which are in the Archivo General de la Nación (Mexico City) and the Archivo General de Indias (Sevilla).

79. Hezeta's biographical details are based on Cutter, "California, Training Ground for Spanish Naval Heroes," *California Historical Society Quarterly*, 40:2, pp.109–22; Thurman, *Naval Department*, pp.141–42.

80. Schurz, *The Manila Galleon*, p.246.

81. Details on ships of the 1775 expedition are based on Kenyon, "Naval Construction at San Blas, Mexico, 1767–1797," pp.114–39; Thurman, *Naval Department*, pp.59–60, 96–97, 145.

82. Kenyon, "Naval Construction," p.131. Moorsom tonnage includes a ship's cubical capacity between upper decks as well as below the main deck. Cook (*Flood Tide*, p.56) says the *Santiago* was a "225-ton craft"; Thurman (*Naval Department*, p.97, n.7) says it "was listed among the records of the naval department at 225 1/2 tons burden." The discrepancy between the tonnages given by Cook and Thurman and Kenyon's figure is explained by the fact that the former are expressed in an 18th-century Spanish unit called a *tonelada de arqueo* ("ton of capacity," which is equal to 53½ cubic feet), while the latter is stated in the modern Moorsom ton (equal to 100 cubic feet). See Kenyon, "Naval Construction," pp.1–45.

83. The Spanish practice of giving ships two names, one official, the other a nickname, has led to some confusion over the name of the *Sonora*. According to Kenyon ("Naval Construction," pp.114, 124) there were two schooners built at San Blas nicknamed *Sonora*. The first, officially named *Nuestra Señora de la Soledad*, sailed to the Philippines in 1767, but proving too small to make the return voyage, this ship had no further involvement in the affairs of San Blas after that time. The second *Sonora*, constructed in 1769 and formally named *Nuestra Señora de Guadalupe*, was the *Santiago*'s consort in 1775. Thurman (*Naval Department*, p.145) says that the *Sonora* used in the Hezeta voyage was also known as the *Felicidad*, and it is implied that the "*Sonora* alias *Nuestra Soñora de Guadalupe*" was a separate ship. See also Thurman, *Naval Department*, p.96.

84. Kenyon, "Naval Construction," p.136.

85. Secondary accounts of the 1775 expedition give the surgeon's name variously as Dávalos (Bancroft, History of the Northwest Coast, vol. 1, p.100) or José Dávila (Wagner, Cartography of the Northwest Coast of America, vol. 1, p.175). Thurman (Naval Department, p.128) says the surgeon aboard the Santiago in 1774 was named José Dávila, but Hezeta's 1775 Diario definitely refers to the surgeon as Juan Gonzales (González in modern spelling).

86. The spelling of the Sonora's second officer's name has been the source of some difficulties. He seems to have always signed his name "Maurelle," which is the spelling generally employed in Hezeta's Diario—except the final "e" is often dropped. The correct spelling of his surname, however, is thought to be "Mourelle," and this is the orthography in general use today. See Mourelle, Voyage of the Sonora in the Second Bucareli Expedition, p.a.

87. See Kenyon, "Naval Construction," p.125; Mourelle, Voyage of the Sonora, p.89.

88. Kenyon (Naval Construction, p.151) says that in addition to its captain and pilot Cañizares, the San Carlos' crew included 48 men. Galvin (The First Spanish Entry into San Francisco, p.3) says its "complement of officers and men numbered 30." There may still have been some overcrowding on the supply ship, as the Hezeta Diario mentions a request by Ayala to transfer some cargo to the Santiago that was on deck and in the crew's way. See entry for 21–22 March.

89. Thurman ("Naval Department," p.126) says the viceroy's instructions of 1774 were "designed for regulating all future explorations from San Blas to the Northwest Coast," and that that was why they were so elaborate. Bucareli's instructions to Hezeta are described in Chapman, The Founding of Spanish California, pp.238–42.

90. The Gaspar de Portolá expedition. See Chapman, The Founding, pp.112–13.

91. Unless, as some argue, Drake entered first in 1579. See Hanna, Lost Harbor, pp.66–78.

92. Greenhow, History of Oregon and California, 4th ed., p.123.

93. See Barrington (trans.) "Journal of a Voyage in 1775," Miscellaines, 2nd ed., pp.469–534; Mourelle, Voyage of the Sonora.

94. For example, See Cook, Flood Tide, pp.78–79.

95 Palóu, Historical Memoirs of New California (trans. by Bolton), vol. 1. p.xcvi.

96. Palóu, Relación historica de la vida y apostólicas tareas de venerable padre fray Junípero Serra.

97. Beaglehole, Journals of Captain James Cook, vol. 3, p.321. Majors ("The Hezeta and Bodega Voyage of 1775," Northwest Discovey, 1:4, p.236) says that a brief no-

tice of the Second Bucareli expedition appeared in the *Gazeta de Madrid* in March, 1776. An English version of this notice next appeared in the *London Evening Post*, 29 May 1776. This was two weeks before Cook sailed from England, and it may have been that to which he referred.

98. Cutter ("Early Spanish Artists on the Northwest Coast," *Pacific Northwest Quarterly*, 2:4, p.153) believes this account may have been authored by José Cardero, artist-cartographer on board the *Mexicana*. *See also* Jane (trans.), *A Spanish Voyage to Vancouver and the Northwest Coast of America*, pp.xxi, 3, 122–23; Turanzas (ed.), *Relación del viage hecho por las goletas Sútil y Mexicana en el año de 1792 para reconnocer el Estrecho de Fuca*, pp.1, 151–58.

99. Humboldt, *Political Essay on the Kingdom of New Spain*, vol. 2, p.363.

100. Humboldt, *Political Essay*, vol. 2, p.365.

101. Greenhow, *History*, p.v.

102. Greenhow, *History*, p.114n.

103. Greenhow, *History*, p.117n.

104. Greenhow, *History*, pp.116–117.

105. Greenhow, *History*, p.123.

106. Greenhow, *History*, p.119.

107. Historia, tomo 324, numero 3, numero 4.

108. Estado, Audiencia de Mexico, legajo 19, documento 11.

109. Greenhow, *History*, pp.430–33. Interestingly enough, Greenhow also says the extract was "copied under the supervision of Don Martin Fernandes de Navarate, the chief of that department [the Madrid Hydrographical Office]." This may have been the same person who published the anonymous account of the *Sútil* and *Mexicana* in 1802.

110. *See* Wagner, "Sierra's Account of the Hezeta Expedition," *California Historical Society Quarterly*, 9:3, pp.201–242; Campa Cos, *A Journal of Exploration: Northward Along the Coast from Monterey . . . 1775*.

# NOTES: HEZETA'S DIARIO

1. The reader would be better advised to *add* the degrees west of San Blas if calculating *west* longitude. The manuscript sources, however, clearly read "will subtract from the longitude of San Blas" (Sp.*substraerá de la longitud de San Blas*). Hezeta evidently intended for his readers to calculate longitude *east* of places such as Tenerife or Paris.

2. The manuscript sources agree on WSW (Sp.OSO), but the correct bearing would seem to be ESE.

3. Don Miguel Manrique.

4. Piedra Blanca (white rock) refers to one of two reefs, today called Piedra Blanca del Mar and Piedra Blanca de Tierra, off the entrance to San Blas. Isabel is a small island about 40 nautical miles NW of San Blas, some 18 nautical miles off the Nayarit coast (lat. 21°52′N; long. 105°54′W). *See* Thurman, *The Naval Department of San Blas*, pp.22, 45.

5. Reinforcing sleeve (Sp.*gimelga*).

6. The Islas Tres Marías is a chain of four islands, three of which bear the names of biblical Marys, running NW-SE, between 60 and 80 nautical miles SW of San Blas. The "SE island of the Marías" is today called Isla María Cleofas. Hezeta observed its latitude at 21°13′N, which is about 3′ below its position on modern charts. *See* Thurman, *Naval Department*, p.45.

7. This island, one of the Revillagigedo group, located about 365 nautical miles SW of San Blas, is today called Socorro.

8. Cortés sent two ships out from Tehuantepec to explore northward along the west coast of Mexico in 1533. One was the *Concepción*, commanded by Diego de Becerra, and the other the *San Lázara*, under Hernando de Grijalva. They became separated, and Grijalva on his own apparently discovered the island Hezeta encountered—but not in 1524. *See* Wagner, *Spanish Voyages to the Northwest Coast of America in the Sixteenth Century*, p.6; Holmes, *From New Spain by Sea to the Californias, 1519–1668*, pp.57–58.

9. It is not clear from these terms which species of birds Hezeta observed.

10. This river, said to have been discovered during the expedition led by Sebastián Vizcaíno in 1602–03, took its name from Martín de Aguilar, captain of the frigate *Tres Reyes*. Aguilar became separated from Vizcaíno's flagship, the *San Diego*, in a storm, and on 19 January 1603, according to Father Antonio de la Ascención, they found themselves in 43°. "Here the land makes a cape or point," his account asserts, "which was named 'Cabo Blanco', and here the coast begins to trend to the northeast. Close to it a copious and deep river was discovered." Its discoverers apparently named it Río de Santa Inéz, but the name Aguilar subsequently prevailed. The identity of this river remains

uncertain, although George Davidson suggested that it might have been the Smith River (lat. 41°56′N) or the Chetko (lat. 42°03′N). He ruled out the Rogue River (lat. 42°25′N) because of its dangerous offshore reefs. Henry Wagner was inclined to think it was the Mad River or Humboldt Bay in the vicinity of 41°N. *See* Wagner, *Spanish Voyages*, pp.255, 407 (n.186), 408 (n.205); Davidson, *Pacific Coast Pilot of California, Oregon and Washington*, p.385.

11. Jacques Nicolas Bellin (1703–72) was a hydrographer in the French Dépôt des Cartes et Plans de la Marine. Throughout the Hezeta manuscript sources he is referred to as M. Bellin or Mr. Bellin, and his maps are continually cited as the expedition's basic—if rather inaccurate—cartographic guide. These references are to Bellin's 1766 *Carte Reduite*, which was apparently copied from a Russian map depicting the discoveries of the Bering-Chirikov expedition of 1741. *See* Wagner, *Cartography of the Northwest Coast of America*, vol. 1. p.178; Beaglehole, *The Journals of Captain James Cook*, vol. 1, p.c (n.2).

12. Based on the latitudes given in Hezeta's Tables for noon of the 8th and 9th of June (41°43′N and 41°14′N respectively) it appears that they made landfall in the vicinity of Point St. George (lat. 41°47′N), and that the expedition was now coasting southward along the gently curving shore that extends down to Rocky Point (lat. 41°08′N).

13. Hezeta mistakenly wrote "Francisco" instead of "Cristóbal."

14. The small peninsula was Trinidad Head (lat. 41°03′N) and they were warping into the cove immediately behind it. Hezeta's Tables give the latitude of the anchorage as 41°06′N. The Indians were probably Yuroks from the village within the cove.

15. The Spanish commonly referred to Indian villages or dwelling places as *rancherías*, a term that has been retained in the translation. The Yurok name of the village was *Tsurai*. *See* Heizer and Mills, *The Four Ages of Tsurai*.

16. The Indians did not disturb the cross, for it was seen by George Vancouver in 1793 and Peter Corney in 1817. Apparently, the cross was first set up on the beach and then later moved to a vantage point on Trinidad Head. *See* Heizer and Mills, *Four Ages*, pp.65, 101, 197 (ns. 34 and 35).

17. There is no indication that the other deserter, José Antonio Rodrigues, returned, and thus he was probably the first European resident of the Northern California coast whose name and manner of arrival is known with certainty. Pérez's account of this episode suggests that Hezeta was much harsher with the natives and Lorenzo than the captain's own version would indicate. Pérez states: "the captain became angered and ordered the men to tie the deserter, and had him given two hundred lashes. All the officers of both ships resented this action, not only because of the punishment of the innocent Indian, but also because the deserter's punishment had been ordered in spite of the captain's having pardoned him the morning he appeared." *See* Heizer and Mills, *Four Ages*, p.55.

18. This river is probably the Little River, which enters the ocean about 2.3 nautical miles SE of Trinidad Head. Francisco Mourelle, pilot of the *Sonora*, says they called the river *Tórtolas* because of seeing a large flock of doves or pigeons. The birds they saw may have been mourning doves (*Zenaida macroura*), which are native throughout most of temperate North America. *See* Mourelle, *Voyage of the Sonora in the Second Bucareli Expedition*, p.32.

19. The Indians in the vicinity of *Río de las Tórtolas*—if it was in fact today's Little River—could have been Wiyot, since the Little River was on the northern periphery of their territory. *See* Kroeber, *Yurok Myths*, p.4.

20. Concerning the reference to bison, Hezeta definitely uses the Spanish word for bison, *cíbolos* (although spelled in the manuscript sources *sibulos*). However, as Heizer and Mills (*Four Ages*, p.196, n.19) suggest, he probably meant elk, since there is no record of bison on the California coast. The word *cíbolo* (fem. *cíbola*) is the same as in the mythical Seven Cities of Cíbola. According to Herbert Bolton (*Spanish Boarderlands*, p.82, n. l) it "is believed to be a Spanish form of the word *Shiwina*, by which the Zuñi called their tribal range."

21. The presence of iron among the Yurok and their evident familiarity with it is a matter of considerable interest. Wagner, in support of his contention that Sir Francis Drake's California anchorage was at Trinidad Harbor, argued that the iron knives may have originated with that event in 1579 (Wagner, *Sir Francis Drake's Voyage Around the World*, p.157). If the explanations reported by Hezeta are taken at face value, however, it is more probable that such materials were obtained indirectly from some unknown shipwreck through trade from the north, or, in at least one case, directly from wreckage that had washed ashore near Trinidad Head. This so-called "drift iron" theory is discussed at length in R. A. Rickard, "The Use of Iron and Copper by the Indians of British Columbia," *British Columbia Historical Quarterly*, 3 : 2, pp.25–50.

22. Heizer and Mills (*Four Ages*, p.196, n.18) believe that these cultivated tobacco plants were the same species as wild tobacco (*Nicotiana begelovii*). It is also possible that the plants mentioned were kinnikinnick (*Arctostaphylos uva-ursi*), which was the principal smoking mixture on the Northwest Coast prior to the introduction of tobacco. In either case, this is probably the earliest mention of smoking as practiced by Northwest Coast Indians—of which the Yuroks were among the southernmost representatives. *See* Gunther, *Ethnobotany of Western Washington*, p.44.

23. These subterranean dwellings were probably sweatlodges. *See* Heizer and Mills, *Four Ages*, p.196, n.24.

24. Probably a reference to the Coast Redwood (*Sequoia sempervirens*).

25. Hezeta's map of Trinidad Harbor shows the location of the *Cañada* about 650 *tuesas* (3,575 ft. or 1,087 meters) SW of Trinidad Head. *Punta Gorda* (fat point) is probably what modern charts call Cape Mendocino. *See* note 64.

26. Hezeta was born in Bilbao on the Cantabrian coast of northern Spain. *See* Cutter, "California, Training Ground for Spanish Naval Heroes," *California Historical Quarterly*, 40:2, p.114.

27. *Aguas malas* refers to the first of the *señas* or signs of land encountered by the navigators of the Manila galleons as they approached the North American coast. Antonio de Morga, in discussing the voyages of these ships across the North Pacific, describes *aguas malas* as "round, purple and as big as a man's hand with a crest in the middle like a lateen sail, called *caravelas*" (*Sucesos de las Islas Filipinas*, p.322). This and Hezeta's description are almost certainly of a jellyfish-type creature called *Velella velella* which is topped with a cellophane-like triangular sail. It is sometimes confused with the Portuguese man-of-war. *See* Ricketts and Calvin, *Between Pacific Tides*, 4th ed., pp.226–27.

28. *Porras*, another of the *señas*, refers to a bulbous-headed, whip-like alga or kelp (*Nereocystis luetkeana*) commonly encountered along the North American coast. Morga (*Sucesos*, p.322) describes them as "very long, hollow, yellow grass-stalks with a ball at the end, floating on the water." *See* Ricketts and Calvin, *Between Pacific Tides*, p.415; Schurz, *The Manila Galleon*, p.239.

29. *Balsas*, another of the *señas*, refers to the vegetative debris carried to sea by coastal streams. *See* Schurz, *Manila Galleon*, p.239.

30. The common murre (*Uria aalge*) is an abundant bird along the west coast of North America, and it feeds at considerable distance from the coast. Hezeta's *centenares* may have been murres. The parrot-like bird he describes is clearly one of two species of puffins, most likely the tufted puffin (*Lunda cirrhata*).

31. The noon observation recorded in Hezeta's Tables for 8 July is 47°03′N, placing the expedition off the Washington coast slightly north of the entrance to Grays Harbor (lat. 46°55′N).

32. The noon observation for 11 July is 48°26′N, placing them almost opposite Cape Flattery (lat. 48°23′N). Mourelle estimated they were 10 leagues (about 30 nautical miles) off shore (*Voyage of the Sonora*, p.70). From such a position, the mountains of Vancouver Island are probably the land that was sighted.

33. A loss of 40′ of latitude from the previous day's noon observation of 48°26′N would have placed the frigate that morning on the Washington coast at about 47°46′N. This is also the latitude of Hoh Head on the Olympic Peninsula, and thus it appears they were within a league (three nautical miles) of that landmark. One of the chaplains, Father Sierra, mentions, in remarking about this unexpectedly close brush with the coast, that "when we awoke we were so near the land we could count the trees." *See* Wagner, "Sierra's Account of the Hezeta Expedition," *California Historical Quarterly*, 9:3, p.226.

34. There has been considerable confusion as to the identification of this point. In the 1840s, Robert Greenhow identified it as Point Grenville (lat. 47°18′N), while George Davidson, four decades later, concluded that it was actually Cape Elizabeth (lat. 47°21′N). Mourelle (*Voyage of the Sonora's*, p.70) gives the latitude of the *Sonora's* anchorage as 47°20′N, which accords well with Davidson's view. Wagner, however, reinvestigated this question in 1933 and, based on a mistaken understanding of the *Santiago's* position in relation to the *Sonora's* and a misreading of Point Grenville's latitude, revived the Greenhow theory. While the question may never be settled to everyone's satisfaction, a recent (1980) reexamination of the evidence by Harry T. Majors suggests convincingly that Davidson was correct in identifying this enigmatic point— later called by the Spanish *Punta de los Mártires* (martyrs' point)—with Cape Elizabeth. The expedition's large-scale map of the vicinity in which the ships anchored also supports the Davidson-Majors thesis. *See* Greenhow, *History of Oregon and California*, 4th ed., p.119; Davidson, *Pacific Coast Pilot*, pp.493–94; Wagner, *Cartography*, vol. 1, p.176; Majors, "The Hezeta and Bodega Voyage of 1775," *Northwest Discovery*, p.212–21, 243–47, n.18.

35. The probable sequence of events on 13 July: The *Sonora* ran in under the lee of Cape Elizabeth at high tide, without realizing the area was shoal. As the tide went out, the dangerous reefs stretching to the south of this cape were revealed and the schooner warned the *Santiago* off. The frigate thereupon turned away, and somewhat later Hezeta "arrived at a small inlet" (Sp.*arribé a una pequeña ensenada*), meaning he went south of the schooner to the bay in the lee of Point Grenville.

36. The surgeon is referred to as Dávalos by Bancroft's writer, Henry L. Oak (Bancroft, *History of the Northwest Coast*, vol. 1, p.100), and Wagner calls him José Dávila (*Cartography*, vol. 1, p.175). According to Donald C. Cutter (*California Coast*, p.215), José Dávila was the name of the *Santiago's* surgeon in 1774 on its voyage from San Blas to San Diego. Cutter says that, because of his "intense fear of the sea," Dávila was replaced at San Diego by Pedro Castán. The Hezeta manuscript sources clearly give the surgeon's name as Juan Gonzales (modern spelling is González), and it is uncertain how Dávila came to be associated with the 1775 voyage.

37. This landing, the first by Europeans on the Northwest Coast south of Alaska for which documentation exists, probably occurred just south of Point Grenville.

38. These Indians were probably Quinaults.

39. Mourelle says the boatswain's name was Pedro Santa Ana (*Voyage*, p.37).

40. If this tragic event occurred in the lee of Cape Elizabeth, as seems likely, it was probably somewhere on the beach just south of the Quinault River.

41. The noon observation for 10 August places the frigate in 49°23′N, so that the land sighted would have been Vancouver Island.

42. If Hezeta's estimated latitudes of these two peaks are accurate, they are probably Victoria Peak (7,095 ft.) in 50°03'N and Golden Hinde (7,218 ft.) in 49°40'N.

43. The latitude observed at noon on 12 August was 49°10'N, placing the *Santiago* at roughly the same latitude as Clayoquot Sound. Because of the NW-SE trend of the coast in this area, however, it is equally conceivable he was referring to Nootka Sound. Another possibility is that Hezeta's "two most prominent capes" (Sp. *los dos cabos más salientes*) were Cape Cook (on the Brooks Peninsula) and Estevan Point (on the Hesquiat Peninsula), which are the two most seaward points of land on Vancouver Island's west coast. The "inlet" (Sp. *ensenada*) formed by these two capes would thus have referred to the 70-mile stretch of coast between them, which is in fact recessed generally between three and four leagues. It is of some interest that when James Cook was off this same coast in 1778, he described two points of land which he called Woody Point (Cape Cook) on the north and Breakers Point (Estevan Point) on the south. "Between these two points," he wrote, "the shore forms a large bay, which I called *Hope Bay*." This suggests that Hezeta's unnamed inlet may indeed have been the same waters to which Cook gave the name Hope Bay. *See* Beaglehole, *The Journals*, vol. 3, pp.294–95.

44. These Indians were Nootka, possibly from Nootka Sound.

45. Sierra says that Hezeta gave the Indians a sabre in exchange for the canoe. *See* Wagner, "Sierra's Account," *California Historical Quarterly*, 9:3, p.234.

46. This appears to be a reference to the two Bodelteh Islands (lat. 48°10'N) and Ozette Island (lat. 48°09'N) off Cape Alava on the northern Washington coast.

47. According to Mourelle (*Voyage*, p.34), this island was discovered by the *Sonora* earlier, on 12 July. It has generally been assumed that the name *Dolores* (sorrows) is connected with the 14 July attack, but neither Hezeta nor Mourelle say so. In fact, if Mourelle is correct in asserting that the island was discovered and named two days before the attack, the island's name could not have been connected with that event. Henry Oak (Bancroft, *Northwest Coast*, vol. 1: p.182, n.21) believed "the name was that of the day on which it was discovered." Mourelle calls the island "barren," which could have been a factor in its naming, although Hezeta describes it as "populated by a dense grove of pine trees" (Sp. *poblada de espesa arboleda de pinos*). This island has been identified with Destruction Island (lat. 47°40'N), but the latitude Hezeta gives for it is 18' too high, being instead very close to the position of James Island (lat. 47°54'N). Today, Destruction Island is largely devoid of trees, while James Island is forested, suggesting that Hezeta may have somehow confused the two. *See* Greenhow, *History*, p.119; Bancroft, *Northwest Coast*, vol. 1, p.160; Davidson, *Pacific Coast Pilot*, p.499; Wagner, *Cartography*, vol. 1, p.176.

48. The feast day of the Assumption of Our Lady (15 August) had just passed, and that presumably was the reason Hezeta named the "bay" *Asunción*. The latitude observed at noon 17 August was 46°11′N, almost exactly the same latitude at which the Columbia River lightship was stationed in the recent past. Hezeta's claim to exactitude, however, may not be warranted entirely, for the ship's location must have been actually somewhere northwest of Cape Disappointment placing its correct latitude in the vicinity of 46°20′N. The map Hezeta refers to depicts a broad bay between 10 and 11 miles (*millas* or Spanish miles) across, extending for fifteen miles eastward off the map. There is little doubt this bay was the estuary of the Columbia River.

49. With this statement, Hezeta has a reasonably valid claim to being the European discoverer of the Columbia River. This claim is all the stronger when one considers that John Meares, 13 years later in 1788, rounded the same northerly cape, naming it Disappointment and its bay Deception, because in his words, "we can now with safety assert that there is no such river as that of San Roc." See Meares, *Voyages Made in the Years 1788 and 1789*, p.168.

50. The manuscript sources definitely state 1692, but the year in which Fuca's voyage is supposed to have occurred—if it did indeed occur—was 1592. The curious story of this apocryphal voyage by one "Juan de Fuca, but properly named Apostolos Valerianus, of nation a Greek, born in Cephalonia, of profession a mariner, and an ancient pilot of ships" was told by an Englishman named Michael Lok the Elder in an account published in 1625. See Greenhow, *History*, pp.408–11; Cook, *Flood Tide*, pp.22–29, 539–43.

51. Hezeta appears to have thought that the northerly cape—Meares' Cape Disappointment—was actually an island, for he so depicts it on the map, and that behind this supposed island lay an anchorage. Although the cape is not in fact an island, it appears to be one when viewed from sea. The cape today shelters the harbor of Ilwaco, Washington.

52. Hezeta's name for the northerly cape, *San Roque*, is believed by Wagner ("Sierra's Account," *California Historical Quarterly*, 9:3, p.235, n.26) to have been in honor of the saint whose feast day was 16 August. Majors ("Hezeta-Bodega Voyage," *Northwest Discovery*, 1:4, p.222), however, asserts that it was named after a Spanish town near Gibralter. There is little doubt that the northerly cape is today's Cape Disappointment (lat. 46°17′N), for its appearance is aptly described by the words "steep, of ruddy earth and little elevated" (*Sp. escarpado, de tierra colorada, con poco elevación*). On the other hand, the cape on the south side that he called *Frondoso* (implying heavy vegetation) is something of a puzzle. Davidson (*Pacific Coast Pilot*, p.456) became convinced that the southerly cape was Tillamook Head (lat. 45°57′N). For the frigate to have sounded in 24 *brazas* (22 fathoms) it would have had to be at least six miles off shore, and thus, Davidson reasoned, Hezeta was too far out to "have noted the low and comparatively unimportant Point Adams." The wide (10 to 11 miles) separation between the two capes on Hezeta's map is further reason to suspect

that *Cabo Frondoso* could not have been Point Adams, which is no more than six nautical miles south of Cape Disappointment. Nevertheless, J. Nielson Barry ("Who Discovered the Columbia River?" *Oregon Historical Quarterly* 39:2, pp.154–55), disregarding Hezeta's sounding of that evening, believed that the frigate was positioned "near where the end of the south jetty is now," placing it well within sight of Point Adams. He attributed the wide separation of the capes shown on the map to the effects of foreshortening. On balance, however, Davidson's view seems more convincing, despite the fact that Tillamook Head is at least 20 nautical miles south of Cape Disappointment.

53. The cape Hezeta named *Falcón* is within 3' of the latitude of the present Cape Falcon (lat. 45°46′N) on the northern Oregon coast, in one of the rare instances where his original toponym has survived on modern charts. Wagner ("Sierra's Account," *California Historical Quarterly*, 9:3, p.235, n.28) says the name probably derives from Santa Clara de Monte Falco, whose feast day is 18 August.

54. The *Santiago* sailed through a shallow section of ocean, part of the continental shelf, that protrudes seaward from 15 to 30 nautical miles off the central Oregon coast between today's Newport and Florence. Northward, it is today called Stonewall Bank. A larger, southerly lobe bears the name Heceta Bank (suggested by George Davidson) in honor of the mariner who first noted the existence of these shallows. *See* Davidson, *Pacific Coast Pilot*, p.408.

55. This "level mountain" (Sp.*una montaña plana*) has never been satisfactorily identified. There is no distinctively flat-topped mountain visible in latitude 45°28′N that would warrant likening it to a table. The land behind the 200- to 400-foot escarpment at Cape Meares (lat. 45°28′N) slopes gently inland to a 1,385-foot unnamed summit, which could have been what Hezeta had in mind. But it is odd that he would use this undistinguished feature as a landfall for Cape Falcon, 18 nautical miles to the north. Greenhow (*History*, p.121) thought *La Mesa* was "Clarke's Point of View," which would locate it on Tillamook Head, implying a major error in the latitude given. If such an error is assumed, 1,900-foot Neahkahnie Mountain (lat. 45°45′N), looming above and just south of Cape Falcon, is probably a better choice as a landfall to mark that cape. But Neahkahnie's summit is more rounded than flat, and so the mystery remains. Davidson and Wagner ventured no opinions on this elusive landmark.

56. Although the Spanish word *islotes* (small islands or islets) is not used to describe these three features, the terms that are used, "headlands or hillocks" (Sp.*farallones o mogotes*), still could mean that they were offshore rocks. Three such rocks, very prominent and distinctive, called the Three Arch Rocks (lat. 45°28′N), are located within 2' of the latitude given for *Las Tres Marías*, and no doubt they are what Hezeta saw. Their location is roughly midway between Tillamook and Netarts bays.

57. *See* note 10.

58. Hezeta was off the Cape Blanco that appears on modern charts at 42°50′N, and which is the westernmost point of the Oregon coast. The small islands he mentions were Blanco Reef, directly off the cape, and Orford Reef, a little farther out and to the south. The channel between them is probably what Hezeta attempted to run—a daring but risky venture for the 225-ton *Santiago*. The modern *United States Coast Pilot* (1968 edition, p.190) says of this channel that, "in clear weather small vessels with local knowledge sometimes use the passage inside Orford Reef and between Orford Reef and Blanco Reef." There are many rocks in this area that are, as Hezeta aptly put it, "level with the sea" (Sp.*rasantes con el mar*).

59. This approach would have brought the *Santiago* into the vicinity of the bight leeward of The Heads (lat. 42°44′N) near Port Orford, Oregon.

60. According to Ascención's account of the Vizcaíno expedition of 1602–03, the flagship *San Diego*, under Vizcaíno's command, was blown northward on 17 January 1603 by a second storm after the one that separated it from the *Tres Reyes* (*see* note 10). The account states that on 19 January, "the eve of the glorious martyr, San Sebastián . . . the wind changed and commenced to blow from the northwest. With this the day cleared up, and on taking the latitude the pilots found themselves in 42°. There was on the coast a cape of white earth close to some high sierras covered with snow. This was named 'Cabo Blanco de San Sebastián'" (Wagner, *Spanish Voyages*, p.253). This was the cape Hezeta appears to have been trying to locate. His noon position of 42°30′N would have put him about 3′ north of the Rogue River Reef (lat. 42°30′N), and the cape he estimated to be in 42°10′N must have been the cape at 42°19′N which today bears the name Sebastian.

61. This is a reference to the Jesuit Father Miguel Venegas, whose work *Noticia de la California* was published in Madrid (1757). *See* Venegas, A *Natural and Civil History of California*, vol. 1, foreword (unpaginated).

62. Although the latitude of Hezeta's *Cabo Diligencias* is 8′ higher than today's Cape Blanco (lat. 42°50′N) there seems little doubt from his description of the offshore islands and channel that these capes must be one and the same. Wagner (*Cartography*, vol. 1, p.177) thought that Bodega y Quadra applied the name *Diligencias* to this cape, but no such claim is made by Bodega in his account of the *Sonora*'s voyage (*First voyage to lat. 58° . . . 1775*). Mourelle mentions seeing a "cape exactly resembling a round table . . . [and] ten small islands, and some others which are scarcely above the sea," but he says nothing of the name *Diligencias*. The Barrington translation of Mourelle's journal gives the latitude of this cape as 45°50′N, although the number "45" may have been a misreading of "42." *See* Mourelle, *Voyage*, p.54.

63. These "three large islets" (Sp.*tres islotes grandes*) are probably the Sisters Rocks (lat. 42°36′N), which are three rocky islets within eight-tenths nautical miles from shore. This location is about midway between Port Orford and the mouth of the Rogue River.

64. The latitude Hezeta gives for this cape is 19' too low for the Cape Mendocino (lat. 40°26'N) on modern charts, but it is within 9' of today's Punta Gorda (lat. 40°15'N). It thus appears that Hezeta's conception of these two closely related landmarks on the northern California coast was the reverse of their modern toponyms, since in June he had given the name *Punta Gorda* to a cape visible from Trinidad that could only have been present day Cape Mendocino. *See* note 25.

65. This apparently is Venegas' *Noticia de la California*.

66. The latitude Hezeta gives for this landfall places it at Bodega Bay, on the central California coast, 16 nautical miles north of Point Reyes (lat. 38°00'N).

67. These breakers were probably along the shoals that extend SE from Bodega Head (38°18'N).

68. These are known as the Farallon Islands, which are located about 25 nautical miles west of the Golden Gate.

69. Ayala and the *San Carlos* had just departed San Francisco Bay three days earlier on 18 September. The letters Hezeta says he found seem to have been left by Fray Vincente Santa María at the foot of a cross at Point Lobo (about 2.5 miles southwest of the Golden Gate). The cross had been set up late in 1774 during a visit there by Fray Francisco Palóu and Fernando Javier de Rivera y Moncado, commander of the presidio at Monterey. *See* Galvin, *The First Spanish Entry into San Francisco Bay*, 1775, p.4.

70. The Punta de los Reyes is no doubt the modern Point Reyes at Drakes Bay, and the Punta de las Almejas (spelled in the manuscript sources *Las Armejas*, meaning "clams") is today's Point San Pedro, south of the Golden Gate facing seaward. *See* Galvin, *First Spanish Entry*, p.101.

71. This probably refers to Point Pinos and New Year's Point.

72. The Channel Islands.

73. The southernmost point of Baja California.

# NOTES: EPILOGUE

1. Wagner, "Sierra's Account of the Hezeta Expedition," in *California Historical Society Quarterly*, 9:3, p.239.

2. Wagner, "Sierra's Account," p.238.

3. Wagner, "Sierra's Account," p.238.

# NOTES: HOW HEZETA NAVIGATED

1. Columbus referred to his venture as La Empresa de las Indias. See Morison, Admiral of the Ocean Sea, p.54.

2. Morison, Admiral, p.194.

3. See Muckelroy, Maritime Archaeology, pp.124–25.

4. See Beaglehole, The Exploration of the Pacific, p.234.

5. Pérez mentions Cabrera Bueno in a summary narrative of his 1774 voyage included in a ms. letter to Viceroy Bucareli dated 31 August 1774.

6. Wagner, Cartography, vol. 1, p.175.

7. Captain Cook also had his share of problems getting accurate latitudes on the Northwest Coast in 1778. His observed latitude of Cape Flattery was seven minutes too low; he was eight minutes under the correct latitude of Estevan Point at Nootka Sound. See Beaglehole, Journals, vol. 3, pp.293–94.

8. There are few instances where the length of Hezeta's league can be reliably gauged against known landmarks. Perhaps the best such opportunity is where he describes the offshore islands at Cape Blanco. Of them, he says they are "about a league and a half distant from the land," remarking later that "the center of these small islands by the cape runs through an angle of 45° of the third [SW] quadrant a distance of two leagues." A league of three nautical miles accords closely with the actual situation of the islands and Hezeta's description of them.

# NOTES: HEZETA'S NAVIGATION TABLES

1. The order of column headings in Hezeta's Navigation Tables varied slightly from month to month. In this version, these minor variations have been made consistent.

2. This is an abbreviation of the full title above the March entries, which reads in full, "Status Comprising the Location of the Frigate on Each Day of the Month of March, 1775." Subsequent tables have similar titles, with substantially the same wording, which have also been abbreviated to state only the month and year. The last table in the series has no title, but it must be for November, since the daily entries correspond to the November dates mentioned in the *Diario*. Column headings are also missing from this last table, although they almost certainly are the same as those in preceding tables.

3. Distances are apparently in nautical miles.

# BIBLIOGRAPHY

## Books

Bancroft, Hubert Howe, Henry. L. Oak, and Frances F. Victor. *History of the Northwest Coast*. 2 vols. San Francisco: A. L. Bancroft & Co., 1884.

Beaglehole, J. C. *The Exploration of the Pacific*. Stanford: Stanford University Press, 1968.

————, editor. *The Journals of Captain Cook on his Voyages of Discovery: The Voyage of the Resolution and Discovery, 1776–1780*. 2 vols. Cambridge: Hakluyt Society, 1967.

Bolton, Herbert E. *Coronado: Knight of Pueblo and Plains*. Albuquerque: University of New Mexico Press, 1949.

————. *The Spanish Borderlands: A Chronicle of Old Florida and the Southwest*. New Haven: Yale University Press, 1921.

Campa Cos, Fray Miguel de la. *A Journal of Exploration Northward Along the Coast from Monterey in the Year 1775*. Edited by John Galvin. San Francisco: John Howell, 1964.

Clarke, S. A. *Pioneer Days of Oregon History*. 2 vols. Portland: J. K. Gill Co., 1905.

Cook, Warren L. *Flood Tide of Empire: Spain and the Pacific Northwest, 1543–1819*. New Haven: Yale University Press, 1973.

Cutter, Donald C. *The California Coast: A Bilingual Edition of Documents from the Sutro Collection*. Translated and edited by George Butler Griffin and Donald C. Cutter. Norman: University of Oklahoma Press, 1969.

Chapman, Charles Edward. *The Founding of Spanish California: The Northward Expansion of New Spain, 1687–1783*. New York: Macmillan Co., 1916.

Davidson, George. *Francis Drake on the Northwest Coast of America in the Year 1579*. Washington: U. S. Government Printing Office, 1887.

————. *Pacific Coast Pilot of California, Oregon and Washington*. 4th ed. Washington: U.S. Government Printing Office, 1889.

Fisher, Raymond. H. *Bering's Voyages: Whither and Why?* Seattle: University of Washington Press, 1977.

Galvin, John, editor. *The First Spanish Entry into San Francisco Bay, 1775*. San Francisco: John Howell, 1971.

Gerhard, Peter. *Pirates on the West Coast of New Spain, 1575–1742.* Glendale, California: Arthur H Clark Co., 1960.

Golder, F. A. *Bering's Voyages: An Account of the Efforts of the Russians to Determine the Relation of Asia and America.* 2 vols. New York: Octagon Books, 1968.

Greenhow, Robert. *History of Oregon and California.* 4th ed. Boston: Freeman and Bolles, 1847.

————, *Memoirs, Historical and Political, on the Northwest Coast of North America, and the Adjacent Territories.* Washington: Blair and Rives, Printers, 1840.

Gunther, Erna. *Ethnobotany of Western Washington.* Seattle: University of Washington Press, 1970.

Hanna, Warren L. *Lost Harbor: The Controversy over Drake's California Anchorage.* Berkeley and Los Angeles: University of California Press, 1979.

Heizer, Robert F. *Elizabethan California.* Ramona, California: Bellena Press, 1974.

————, ed. *Handbook of North American Indians, California.* Vol. 8. Washington, D.C.: Smithsonian Institution, 1978.

————, and John E. Mills. *The Four Ages of Tsurai: A Documentary History of the Indian Village on Trinidad Bay.* Translation of Spanish documents by Donald C. Cutter. Berkeley and Los Angeles: University of California Press, 1952.

Hodge, Fredrick W., Theodore H. Lewis, editors. *Spanish Explorers in the Southern United States, 1528–1543.* New York: Barnes and Noble, 1977.

Holmes, Maurice G. *From New Spain by Sea to the Californias, 1519–1668.* Glendale, California: Arthur H. Clark Co., 1963.

Humboldt, Baron Alexander von. *Political Essay on the Kingdom of New Spain.* 5 vols. Translated by John Black. London: Longman, Hurst, Rees, Orme, and Brown, 1811 (AMS Reprint, New York, 1966).

Jane, Cecil, translator. *A Spanish Voyage to Vancouver and the Northwest Coast of America.* London: Argonaut Press, 1930.

Kelly, Celsus OFM, translator and editor. *La Austrialia Del Espíritu Santo.* 2 vols. Cambridge: Hakluyt Society, 1966.

Kroeber, A. L. *Yurok Myths.* Berkeley and Los Angeles: University of California Press, 1978.

La Pérouse, Jean Francois Galaup de. *A Voyage Round the World Performed in the Years 1785, 1786, 1787, 1788 by the Boussole and Astrolabe.* 2 vols. London: Robinson, Edwards and Payne, 1799.

Mathes, W. Michael. *Vizcaino and Spanish Expansion in the Pacific Ocean, 1580–1630.* San Francisco: California Historical Society, 1968.

Meares, John. *Voyages Made in the Years 1788 and 1789 from China to the North West Coast of America.* London: Logographic Press, 1790.

Morga, Antonio de. *Sucesos de las Islas Filipinas.* Translated and edited by J. S. Cummins. Cambridge: Hakluyt Society, 1971.

Morison, Samuel Eliot. *Admiral of the Ocean Sea: A Life of Christopher Columbus.* Boston: Little Brown and Co., 1942.

————. *The European Discovery of America: The Southern Voyages, AD 1492–1616.* New York: Oxford University Press, 1974.

Mourelle, Francisco Antonio. *Voyage of the Sonora in the Second Bucareli Expedition.* Edited by Thomas C. Russell. Translated by Daines Barrington. San Francisco: Thomas C. Russell, 1920.

Muckelroy, Keith. *Maritime Archaeology.* Cambridge: Cambridge University Press, 1978.

Palóu, Fray Francisco. *Historical Memoir of New California.* 4 vols. Translated by Herbert E. Bolton. Berkeley: University of California Press, 1926.

————. *Relación historica de la vida y apostólicas tareas del venerable padre fray Junipero Serra.* Mexico City: Felipe de Zúñiga y Ontiveros, 1787 (Readex Microfilm reprint, 1966).

Penzer, N. M., editor. *The World Encompassed and Analogous Contemporary Documents Concerning Sir Francis Drake's Circumnavigation of the World.* New York: Cooper Square Publishers, 1969.

Ricketts, Edward F., and Jack Galvin. *Between Pacific Tides.* 4th ed. Revised by Joel W. Hedgepth. Stanford: Stanford University Press, 1969.

Ruby, Robert H., and John A. Brown. *The Chinook Indians: Traders of the Lower Columbia River.* Norman: University of Oklahoma Press, 1976.

Schurz, William Lytle. *The Manila Galleon.* New York: E. P. Dutton & Co., 1959.

Smith, Frances Rand. *The Architectural History of Mission San Carlos Borromeo, California.* Berkeley: California Historical Survey Commission, 1921.

Swift, Jonathan. *Gulliver's Travels.* Baltimore: Penguin Books, 1972.

Thurman, Michael E. *The Naval Department of San Blas: New Spain's Bastion for Alta California and Nootka, 1767–1798.* Glendale, California: Arthur H. Clark Co., 1967.

Turanzas, José Porrua, editor. *Relación del viage hecho por las goletas Sútil y Mexicana en el año de 1792 para reconocer el Estrecho de Fuca.* Madrid: Artes Gráficas Minerva, 1958.

Udvardy, Miklos D.F. *The Audubon Society Field Guide to North American Birds, Western Region.* New York: Alfred A. Knopf, 1977.

*United States Coast Pilot, No. 7 Pacific Coast: California, Oregon, Washington, and Hawaii.* 10th Edition. Washington, D.C.: U.S. Government Printing Office, 1968.

Vancouver, George. *A Voyage of Discovery to the North Pacific Ocean and Round the World . . . Performed in the Years 1790 . . . 1795.* 6 vols. London: John Stockdale, 1801.

Venegas, Miguel. *A Natural and Civil History of California.* 2 vols. London: James Rivington and James Fletcher, 1759 (Readex Microfilm reprint, 1966).

Wagner, Henry R. *Cartography of the Northwest Coast of America to the Year 1800.* 2 vols. Berkeley: University of California Press, 1937 (N. Isreal reprint, 1968).

————. *Sir Francis Drake's Voyage Around the World: Its Aims and Achievements.* San Francisco: John Howell, 1926.

————. *Spanish Voyages to the Northwest Coast of America in the Sixteenth Century.* San Francisco: California Historical Society, 1929 (N. Isreal reprint, 1966).

## Articles

Barrington, Daines (trans.). "Journal of a Voyage in 1775," in *Miscellanies* (London, 1781) pp.469–543.

Barry, J. Neilson. "Who Discovered the Columbia River?"*Oregon Historical Quarterly* 39 (1938): 152–61.

Beals, Herbert K., and Harvey Steele. "Chinese Porcelains from Site 35-TI-1, Netarts Sand Spit, Tillamook County, Oregon." *University of Oregon Anthropolical Papers* No. 23, 1981.

Bishop, R. P. "Drake's Course in the North Pacific." *British Columbia Historical Quarterly* 3 (1939): 151–82.

Cutter, Donald C. "California, Training Ground for Spanish Naval Heroes." *California Historical Society Quarterly* 40 (1961): 109–122.

————. "Early Spanish Artists on the Northwest Coast." *Pacific Northwest Quarterly* 54 (1963): 150–57.

————. "Spain and the Oregon Coast." In *The Western Shore: Oregon Country Essays Honoring the American Revolution*. Edited by Thomas Vaughan. Portland: Oregon Historical Society, 1975.

Heizer, Robert Fleming. "Archaeological Evidence of Sebastian Rodríguez Cermeño's California Visit in 1595." *California Historical Society Quarterly* 20 (1941): 315–28.

Holmes, Kenneth L. "Francis Drake's Course in the North Pacific, 1579." *The Geographical Bulletin* 17 (June 1979).

Majors, Harry M. "The Hezeta amd Bodega Voyage of 1775." *Northwest Discovery* 1 (1980): 208–52.

Rickard, T. A. "The Use of Iron and Copper by the Indians of British Columbia." *British Columbia Historical Quarterly* 3 (1939): 25–50.

Servin, Manuel P., translator. "The Instructions of Viceroy Bucareli to Ensign Juan Pérez." *California Historical Society Quarterly* 40 (1961): 237–48.

Stafford, O. F. "The Wax of Nehalem Beach." *Oregon Historical Quarterly* 9 (1908): 24–41.

Wagner, Henry R., editor, and A. J. Baker, translator. "Fray Benito de la Sierra's Account of the Hezeta Expedition to the Northwest Coast in 1775." *California Historical Society Quarterly* 9 (1930): 201–42.

## Unpublished Sources

Bodega y Quadra, Juan Francisco de la. "First voyage to lat. 58° in a schooner of 18 cubits keel and 6 beam, manned by a pilot, a boatswain, a mate, ten seamen, a cabin boy and a servant, 1775." Translated by G. F. Barwick, 1911. (Typescript copy in the British Columbia Provincial Archives at Victoria.)

Hezeta y Dudagoitia, Bruno de. "Diario de la Navegación hecha por el Teniente de Navío de la Real Armada Don Bruno de Hezeta a explorar la costa septentrional de Californias. Año de 1775." Historia vol. 324, nos. 3 & 4, in Archivo General de la Nación (Ciudad Mexico); legajo 19, documento 11, in Archivo General de Indias (Sevilla). (Microfilm copies in the manuscript collection, Oregon Historical Society, Portland.)

Kenyon, Malcolm H. "Naval Construction and Repair at San Blas, Mexico, 1767–1797." Master's thesis, History, University of New Mexico, Albuquerque, New Mexico, nd.

Newman, Thomas. "Tillamook Prehistory and Its Relation to the Northwest Coast Culture Area." Ph.D. diss., Anthropology, University of Oregon, Eugene, 1959.

Pérez Hernández, Juan Joseph. Letters to Viceroy Bucareli dated 31 August and 3 November, 1774. Estado 38A-3; Archivo General de Indias (Sevilla). (Microfilm copies in the manuscript collection, Oregon Historical Society, Portland.)

———. "Continuación del Diario que formó el Alferez graduado de Fragata Dn. Juan Pérez, Primer Piloto del Departamento de Sn. Blas, con la titulada Santiago, alias la Nueva Galicia de su mando, que comprehende su salida de Monterrey a explorar la Costa Septentrional, y su regreso a este propio Puerto en 26 de Agosto de este año de 1774." Estado 38A-3, Archivo General de Indias (Sevilla). (Microfilm copies in the manuscript collection, Oregon Historical Society, Portland.)

# INDEX

decision not to cross bar of, 88–89, 109; Hezeta's discovery of, 43, 86, 145n.49; lightship, 145n.48. *See also* Asunción, Bahía de la, Deception Bay and Hezeta, Entrada de

Columbus, Christopher, 2, 103–104

*Concepción* (ship), 6–7, 139n.8

*Content* (ship), 18

Cook, Cape, 144n.43

Cook, James, 39–40, 150n.7; discovery of Nootka Sound, 43; off Vancouver Island in 1778, 144n.43; third voyage of, 103

Coronado. *See* Vázquez de Coronado, Francisco

Corrientes, Cabo, 17

Corsairs: English, 17, 25; Dutch, 25

Cortés, Hernando, 6–8

Crespi, Fray Juan, 99; diary of 1774 voyage, 40–42

Cruz, Situación de la, 74–75

Cuchillada de Roldán, 82. *See also* Golden Hinde

Culiacán, Mexico, 6–7

Cutter, Donald C., 11, 44, 143n.36

Davidson, George, 140n.10, 146n.55; identifies Cabo Frondoso as Tillamook Head, 146n.52; identifies Punta de los Mártires as Cape Elizabeth, 143n.34; suggests name of Heceta Bank, 146n.54

Dávila (Dávalos), José: mistakenly identified as *Santiago's* surgeon in 1775, 139n.85; surgeon on part of *Santiago's* 1774 voyage, 143n.36

"Dead reckoning": defined, 104

Deception Bay: John Meares' name for Columbia River estuary, 145n.49. *See also* Columbia River

Depósito Hidrográfico (Museo Naval, Madrid), 42

Dépôt des Cartes et Plans de la Marine (Paris), 58–59, 140

Desembarco, Isla del, 74–75

*Desire* (ship), 18

Destruction Island: devoid of trees, 144n.47; identified as Isla Dolores, 144n.47. *See also* Dolores, Isla

Diligencias, Cabo, 39, 92, 110; identified as Cape Blanco, 147n.62. *See also* Blanco, Cape

Disappointment, Cape, 86, 145n.48–52. *See also* San Roque, Cabo de

Dixon Entrance, 26, 31

Dolores, Isla: described by Hezeta, 85, 144n.47; described by Mourelle, 144n.47; discovered by *Sonora*, 144n.47; Hezeta's position of, close to James Island, 144n.47; identified as Destruction Island, 144n.47; origin of name, 144n.47. *See also* Destruction Island and James Island

Drake, Sir Francis, 6, 15–16, 20–21, 25, 31, 37

Drakes Bay, 11, 19, 21. *See also* San Francisco, Bahía de

"Drift iron." *See* Iron

Elizabeth, Cape, 143n.40; identified as Punta de los Mártires, 74. *See also* Mártires, Punta de los

*El Toisón* (ship). *See San Carlos*

Emeralds: mentioned by Cabeza de Vaca, 7

*Encarnación* (ship), 25

Engaño, Isla del, 75; identified as Grenville Arch, 74

England, 18, 103

Entrada de Hezeta. *See* Hezeta, Entrada de

*Espíritu Santo* (ship), 25

Esteban, Antonio, 3, 95, 99–100

Estevan Point, 144n.43; Cook's observed latitude of, 150n.7. *See also* Breakers Point

Falcón, Cabo, 89; location of, 146n.53; origin of name, 146n.53. *See also* Falcon, Cape

Falcon, Cape, 146 n.53, n.55; latitude of, 107. *See also* Falcón, Cabo

Farallon Islands, 95–96, 148 n.68

Fish: red gurnard, 76; salmon, 76; sardines, 71

Flattery, Cape, 142 n.32; Cook's observed latitude of, 150 n.7

Florence, Oregon, 146 n.54

Food: acorns, 20; hazelnuts, 20; jerked beef, 71; thistles, 20

Frondoso, Cabo, 86, 89; identified as Point Adams, 146 n.52; identified as Tillamook Head, 145 n.52. *See also* Adams, Point, and Tillamook Head

Fuca, Juan de, 18, 88, 145 n.50

*Gazeta de Madrid*: notice of second Bucareli expedition in, 137–38 n.97

Gibralter, 145 n.52; Strait of, 2

Gold, 7, 18. *See also* Trade: commodities in Manila-Acapulco

Golden Gate, 11, 19, 23, 148 n.68–70

*Golden Hind* (ship), 15

Golden Hinde (mountain): Hezeta's sighting of, 82, 144 n.42; latitude of, 107. *See also* Cuchillada de Roldán

Gonzales, Juan, 35, 76; certifies number of sick crewmen, 79; mentioned as surgeon on *Santiago's* 1775 voyage, 143 n.36

Gonzales Cabrera Bueno, Joseph, 104; mentioned by Pérez in letter to Bucareli, 150 n.5

Gorda, Punta, 71, 92, 141 n.25, 148 n.64; latitude of, 107. *See also* Mendocino, Cape, and Mendocino, Cabo

Gray, Robert, 3, 41

Grays Harbor, 142 n.31

Great Armada (Spanish), 18

Grenville, Point: Hezeta's landing near, 143 n.37; latitude of, 107, 112

Greenhow, Robert, 41–43; identifies La Mesa as "Clarke's Point of View,"

146 n.55; identifies Punta de los Mártires as Point Grenville, 143 n.34

Grenville Arch, 74. *See also* Engaño, Isla de

Grenville Bay, 74, 110

Grijalva, Hernando de, 6, 56, 139 n.8

Guam, 13

Guatulco, Mexico, 8, 15–16

Guzmán, Nuño de, 6–7

Heceta. *See* Hezeta y Dudagoitia, Bruno de

Heceta Bank, 146 n.54

Hesquiat Peninsula, 144 n.43

Hezeta, Entrada de, 41, 86. *See also* Asunción, Bahía de la, and Columbia River

Hezeta-Bodega expedition. *See* Bucareli expedition, second

Hezeta expedition. *See* Bucareli expedition, second

Hezeta y Dudagoitia, Bruno de, 34–37, 51, 65, 75, 86, 99–100, 103–104, 107, 109, 112–13; arrives in Mexico, 33; biographical details of, 33; diary of, discussed, 5, 44, 47; diary of, illustrated, 45–46; discovers Columbia River, 43, 86, 145 n.49; Greenhow's opinion of, 39, 43; lands at Rada de Bucareli, 76; proposal of, to colonize Trinidad Harbor, 72–73. *See also* Bucareli expedition, second

Hoh Head, 142 n.33

Hope Bay: Cook's name for inlet on Vancouver Island, 144 n.43

Humboldt, Baron Alexander von, 41–43

Humboldt Bay, 23, 140 n.10

Hydrographic Office (Madrid). *See* Depósito Hidrográfico

Ilwaco, Washington, 145 n.51

Indians, 43, 62–65; attack *Sonora's*

Point Grenville, 143 n.34. *See also* Elizabeth, Cape, and Grenville, Point

Maurelle. *See* Mourelle, Francisco Antonio

Meares, Cape, 146 n.55

Mendocino, Cape, 5, 11, 14, 19, 21–22, 25, 141 n.25, 148 n.64. *See also* Mendocino, Cape, and Gorda, Punta

Mendoza, Antonio de (viceroy of New Spain, 1535–50), 8–9

Mendoza y Luna, Juan de. *See* Montesclaros, marqués de

*Mexicana* (ship), 40

Mexico, 3, 6–8, 15–17, 24, 33, 104

Mexico, Gulf of, 6

Mexico City, 8, 20, 25–26, 40; archives at, 44

Miwok Indians: provide food for Cermeño's crew, 20; sites of, at Drakes Bay, 20

Monterey, 26, 30–31, 35–36, 39–40, 43, 61, 70, 93, 95–96, 100; latitude of harbor, 107; map of harbor at, 28–29; presidio at, 99, Vizcaíno's proposal to colonize, 23–24. *See also* Monterey Bay

Monterey, conde de, Gaspar de Zúñiga y Acevedo (viceroy of New Spain, 1595–1603), 20–21, 23

Monterey Bay, 3, 11, 15, 21, 93; depths of 45 fathoms found at, 132 n.23; map of, 28–29

Montesclaros, marqués de, Juan de Mendoza y Luna (viceroy of New Spain, 1603–7), 23–24

Moorsom ton, 34–35; explained, 136 n.82

Morison, Samuel Eliot, 7–8, 11, 103

Morro Bay, 17

Mourelle [or Maurelle], Francisco Antonio, 35, 40, 42, 61–62, 65, 74, 96, 110, 141 n.18, 142 n.32, 147 n.62; diary of 1775 voyage, 39; orthography of name, 137 n.86

Moya de Contreras, Pedro, archbishop and visitador (viceroy of New Spain, 1584–85), 16–17

*Naos de China*. *See* Manila galleons

Navarrete, Martín Fernández de, 40, 42

Navidad, Mexico, 9, 12, 14

Navigation: celestial, 103; "dead reckoning," 104; instruments, 103–106, 109

Nayarit (state), Mexico, 26, 27

Neahkahnie Mountain, 146 n.55

Nehalem sand spit, 135 n.69

New Mexico, 8, 73

Newport, Oregon, 146 n.54

New Spain, 8, 12, 16, 18–23, 26

New Year's Point, 148 n.71

Nootka Sound, 31, 43, 144 n.43, n.44, 150 n.7

North America, 5, 9, 12–13, 31, 33; Manila galleons' approach to, 14

Northwest Coast (of America), 3, 39–40, 58–59; first map of, based on discoveries of second Bucareli expedition, 110–11

Nova Albion, 6, 16. *See also* Alta California and California

*Nuestra Señora de Esperanza* (ship), 17

*Nuestra Señora de Guadalupe* (ship). *See Sonora*

*Nueva Galicia* (ship). *See Santiago*

Núñez Cabeza de Vaca, Alvar, 7–8

Oak, Henry L., 9, 143 n.36

Olympic Mountains, 31

Olympic Peninsula, 37, 142 n.33

Oregon: central coast of, 31, 146 n.54; northern coast of, 146 n.53; shipwrecks and castaways on northern coast of, 135 n.69; southern coast of, 11, 25, 107, 112; western most extension of, 146 n.58

145 n.48; Most Holy Trinity, 63; of Indians at Trinidad Harbor, 70

Revilla, Cristobal de, 35, 43, 61–63, 76, 78, 80, 88; statement of, 82

Revilla Gigedo, conde de, Juan Vincente de Güemes Pacheco de Padilla (viceroy of New Spain, 1789–94), 111

Revillagigedo, Islas de, 6

Reyes, Point, 11, 19, 22, 148 n.66. See also Reyes, Punta de los

Reyes, Punta de los, 22, 96; identified as Point Reyes, 148 n.70. See also Reyes, Point

Rica de Oro, 17, 24

Rica de Plata, 17, 24

Roca Partida, 53

Rocky Point, 19, 140 n.12

Rodrigues, José Antonio: desertion of, at Trinidad Harbor, 64, 140 n.17

Rodríguez Cabrillo, Juan, 9, 11–12, 14–15, 21, 24

Rodríguez Cermeño, Sebastián, 19–22

Rogue River, 23, 140 n.10

Rogue River Reef, 140 n.10, 147 n.60

Rosario (ship), 25

Russians: map mentioned depicting Bering-Chirikov discoveries, 140 n.11; maritime expeditions to North America, 26; sovereignty in northwestern America, 26; sovereignty in Siberia, 25. See also Siberia

St. George, Point, 19, 140 n.12

St. George (ship), 25

St. Petersburg, Russia, 25; Imperial Academy of, 61

San Agustin (ship), 19–20, 22

San Blas, Mexico, 3, 30, 33–34, 39, 51–53, 56–57, 96, 104, 106; map of, 27; Naval Department of, established, 26; shipyards, 34

San Buenaventura (ship), 20

San Carlos Borromeo, Mission of, 40, 86, 95; ground plan of, 94; stone church at, 99

San Carlos (El Toisón) (ship), 34–36, 51–53; departure from San Francisco Bay, 148 n.69; locates Golden Gate, 39

San Diego, 8, 15, 26, 31, 53, 143 n.36. See also San Diego Bay

San Diego Bay, 9; map of, 27

San Diego (ship), 21–22, 139 n.10, 147 n.60. See also San Miguel (harbor)

San Filipe (ship), 33

San Francisco, Bahía de, 19. See also Drakes Bay

San Francisco, Puerto de, 21, 36, 93, 95–96

San Francisco Bay, 12, 33; charting of, 35; first maritime entrance into, 39; Hezeta's visit to, 95

San Francisco Xavier (ship), 25; uncertainty of last sailing date, 135 n.69

San Lázaro (ship), 6, 139 n.8

San Lucas, Cabo, 8–9, 17, 21, 25, 96

San Lucas, Puerto de, 17

San Miguel (harbor), 9. See also San Diego Bay

San Miguel (island), 11, 14–15

San Pablo (ship), 14

San Pedro, Point: identified as Punta de las Almejas, 148 n.70

San Pedro y Pablo (ship), 24

San Roque, Cabo de, 86; appearance of, 89; identified as Cape Disappointment, 145 n.52; origin of name, 145 n.52. See also Cape Disappointment

San Roque, Spain, 145 n.52

San Salvador (ship), 9

San Sebastián, Cape, 5. See also Sebastian, Cape, and Blanco de San Sebastián, Cabo

San Sebastián (saint), 147 n.60

Santa Ana, Pedro: boatswain on Sonora, 143 n.39

Santa Ana (ship), 17–19